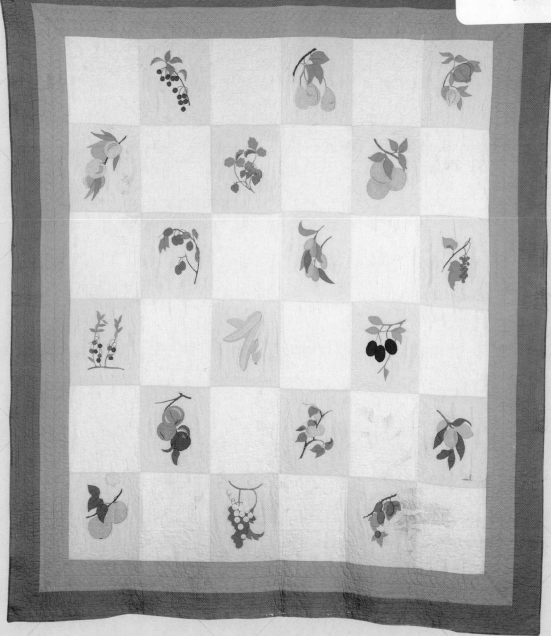

"Horn of Plenty"
69" x 78"
Made by Madeline Narron, dated 1932.
Owned by Deanna Spencer, Overland Park, KS.

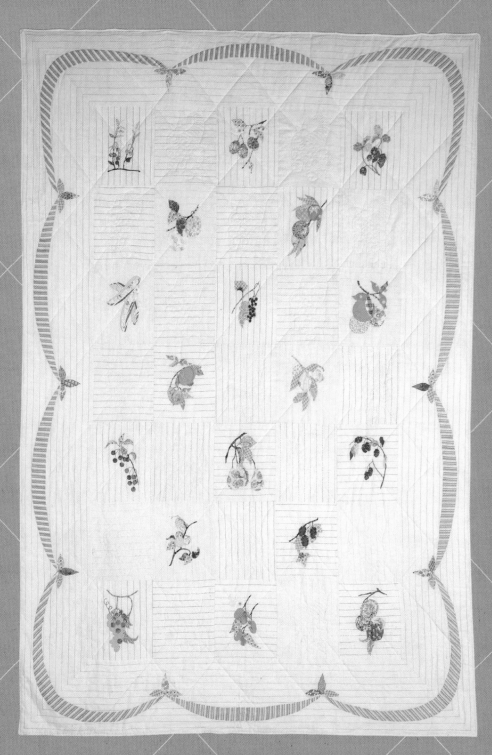

"Deja Vu"
70"x 103"
Made by Tresa Jones, Seneca, KS, 2004.
Tresa used no reproduction fabrics making this quilt.

HORN OF PLENTY

For a New Century

By Kathy Delaney

KANSAS CITY STAR BOOKS

ACKNOWLEDGEMENTS

It is so important to remember nothing we do of any consequence is ever done totally independent of assistance. Without the help of many, this book would not have been possible and I thank each and every contributor.

First and foremost, I thank Doug Weaver for the opportunity to share with you these patterns and projects. I offer many thanks to Edie McGinnis and Judy Pearlstein for their keen eyes and editing abilities, to Jo Ann Groves for her magic with my instructional photographs and Bill Krzyzanowski for his magic in the photography studio. I thank Vicky Frenkel for once again putting it all together with such flair.

Jeanne Poore introduced the original collection of fruit patterns by Eveline Foland to me, for which I am very grateful. I appreciate Barbara Brackman for giving me insight into the designer and her time in history.

Thank you, Carol Kirchhoff, owner of Prairie Point Quilts in Shawnee, Kansas, for your encouragement and support during this process. You and my fellow staff members of Prairie Point are special family!

The Legler Barn Quilters: Jean Arnold, Phillys Bartels, C.J. Cook, Allison Ellliott, Merry Feagins, Sally Kennedy, Sue Locker, LaDonna Marks, Conny Miller, Elaine Pegram, Ann Piette, Mary Strege, Pat White and especially Lang Davis, Linda Mooney, Jeanne Poore and Wava Stoker who put in most of the 500 hours of quilting on my "Horn of Plenty for a New Century" quilt — without you, there would have been no quilt by the publishing date!

Thank you, Connie Coffman, Gloria Donohue, Barb Fife and Kim Morrow for testing the project patterns and making the samples. Cathy Audley, Kathy Berner, Donna Howard, Tresa Jones, Linda Kilpatrick, Linda Mooney, Jeanne Poore, Emily Senuta and Susan Winnie took the appliqué patterns to make samples for the gallery and chapter photographs. I am so grateful for your generosity of time! Thank you, Deanne Spencer, for sharing your grandmother's original quilt, made in the 1930's.

Last, but certainly not least, thank you, reader, for purchasing this book and making it part of your quilting library. May the sweetness of fruit fill all of your quilting days!

HORN OF PLENTY
for a new century

by Kathy Delaney

Editor: Edie McGinnis
Copy Editor: Judy Pearlstein
Design: Vicky Frenkel
Photography: Bill Krzyzanowski
Production Assistant: Jo Ann Groves
Instructional photos and graphics by Kathy Delaney
Antique items courtesy of Edie McGinnis, Kansas City, Missouri.

Published by Kansas City Star Books
1729 Grand Blvd., Kansas City, Missouri, 64108
All rights reserved
Copyright© 2004 by The Kansas City Star Co.

First Edition, first printing
Library of Congress Control Number:
ISBN: 0-9754804-2-1

Printed in the United States of America by Walsworth Publishing Co.

To order copies, call StarInfo (816-234-4636)

www.PickleDish.com

TABLE OF CONTENTS

ABOUT THE AUTHOR

Kathy cannot remember exactly when she began sewing but she can remember her first sewing machine. It was a "toy" that actually sewed and she made crude clothing for her dolls. Eventually she graduated to her mother's Featherweight and then to her mother's new Singer. (Unfortunately the Featherweight was traded in for the new machine at a time when Singer was destroying the old to make way for the new!) Eventually Kathy graduated from very simple clothing to tailored coats for herself and suits for her husband. In 1991 she met her first quilt and can count on one hand the number of garments she has made in the years since!

Since playing "school" at a very young age (her dolls and dog were her students), Kathy has been a teacher. She loves sharing what she knows with anyone who wishes to learn. What better venue to share quiltmaking knowledge than teaching quilt groups around the country and writing books about quiltmaking? Next to actually making quilts, Kathy's favorite activity is teaching others to make quilts.

Kathy lives in Overland Park, Kansas, with Rich Delaney, her husband of 32 years. At this writing, her older son, Sean, and his new wife are members of the United States Army. Her younger son, Ian, is a member of the Arizona Repertory Theater at the University of Arizona where he is in the acting program.

INTRODUCTION

Several years ago I picked up a copy, hot off the presses, of the second in the series of quilt books from Kansas City Star Books, "Star Quilts II - More of the Legendary Kansas City Star Quilt Patterns." Besides an array of historical piecing patterns that appeared in The Kansas City Star newspaper between 1931 and 1955, I discovered the most intriguing collection of appliqué patterns that I was compelled to transform into fabric. The 20 patterns first appeared in the newspaper between October 13, 1930, and November 7, 1930, and were designed by Eveline Foland and signed with her very distinctive signature. I was immediately drawn to the quilt patterns, not only because of the simplicity of the flowers, but by the dates. My older son's birthday is October 13 and my younger son was born November 7, four years later. What fun I had making that quilt!

Once I had completed the quilt, with much satisfaction I might add, my good friend Jeanne Poore introduced me to a second series of appliqué patterns that appeared in The Kansas City Star, between January 5, 1932, and February 24, 1932, by the same designer. I fell in love with the array of fruit designs and was inspired! This time I decided I would make a few changes to suit my style of work. Where Eveline Foland's designs relied on embroidery to define some of the elements of her designs, I decided to add my own touches by redrawing the patterns to substitute appliqué for the embroidery. I was able to make some of those elements, such as fine stems, actually stitchable by increasing the size of the patterns so each one filled the background block equally. The original patterns varied in size even though the background size was uniform throughout.

Within these pages you will find both Ms. Foland's original patterns and my version for your stitching delight. Tresa Jones of Seneca, Kansas, made her quilt true to the original, even using vintage fabric from the period while my quilt is replete with my own hand dyed fabrics as well as commercial batik fabrics and contemporary prints. Don't feel these patterns should be limited to appliqué. Notice in the Gallery the patterns have been used to demonstrate a wide variety of techniques including embroidery, chenille, trapunto, Spanish Blackwork, bobbin drawing and machine quilting. My hope is you will find inspiration and try these patterns in your favorite techniques. Whether you choose one of the projects presented or create your own, keep in mind fruit is good for you!

Who was Eveline Foland?

Eveline Foland (pronounced Eva-leen) was one of just three quilt-pattern designers whose work appeared in The Kansas City Star newspaper between 1928 and 1962. Not very much is known about Ms. Foland actually. She began as an illustrator, most often in fashion or home decoration. Her first quilt pattern appeared in March of 1929. It wasn't until August of 1930 her patterns appeared exclusively. Before that, her patterns were often mixed in with patterns developed by Ruby McKim Studios. While Ms. Foland's signature appeared on 131 quilt patterns in the paper, most were illustrations of traditional patterns readers had sent in. Ms. Foland actually designed only a few patterns and is best remembered for the series designs she created, of which "Horn of Plenty" is one.

Eveline Foland often included very sketchy directions with the patterns. She usually only suggested a fabric choice be "light" or "dark," leaving the quilter to decide color. The directions for making her early patterns often included mistakes or were misleading or incomplete but her skills and understanding of the quilt making process rapidly improved.

Eveline Foland developed three series patterns for quilts. The first appeared in December 1929 and was called "Santa's Parade in a Nursery Quilt." It was developed as a design for embroidery and may very well have been inspired by an inventive marketing campaign which took place November 1929 through The Kansas City Star owned radio station, WDAF. The advertising campaign hailed a visit by Santa Claus to Kansas City on the starting day of the first big shopping weekend of the

holiday season. It was announced that Santa would ride in a big parade through downtown Kansas City and would be joined by such characters as Little Crystal, the fairy, the controversial Punch and Judy puppet characters, Jack in the Box and other familiar nursery rhyme characters. These patterns have been reprinted in a book by Jeanne Poore, "Santa's Parade of Nursery Rhymes," published by Kansas City Star Books in 2000. "Santa's Parade" was followed by the "Memory Bouquet" series in 1930 and "Horn of Plenty" in 1932.

By the end of 1932 it appeared Eveline Foland was no longer with The Kansas City Star. While a few patterns with her signature appeared after 1932, they were probably reprints of previously published patterns. Her last, and rather complicated pattern, "Pilot's Wheel," was incomplete and was followed on February 21 and March 1, 1933, by a reprint, complete with a title and piecing illustration for the block. Ms. Foland's departure remains a mystery, as no information about her can be found. It is believed by some that Ms. Foland may have moved to Chicago and was remarried, changing her name. There is no doubt that her short time as quilt pattern illustrator greatly influenced the quilt making of many midwestern quilters during the 1930's.

"Horn of Plenty for a New Century"
83" x 80"
Made by Kathy Delaney, Overland Park, KS;
quilted by The Legler Barn Quilters, Lenexa, KS, 2004.

CHAPTER 1
Appliqué Basics

The style of appliqué that I employ is needleturn. This means I use my needle to turn under the seam allowance as I am stitching. I find this to be the most efficient method, as it requires no extra steps in seam allowance preparation or basting before stitching to the background.

Every appliqué artist has his/her own set of favorite methods. Those methods will dictate the supplies used. Since I work in a quilting supply store, I have the opportunity to try more gadgets than the average quilter. I try many different techniques before I settle on what works best - for me. On these pages I will be sharing with you just that, what works best for me. I hope you will give these ideas a try. They just may be what works best for you, too.

1-1

Pattern

You will notice the patterns within these pages are full-sized line drawings of the blocks. I think you have much more success if you begin with a full-sized drawing rather than trying to fit individual templates together. If you draw the templates as a complete "picture" and then cut them apart, the shared lines will be more accurate. You won't find any individual templates for the blocks of the Horn of Plenty patterns.

Fabric

If you haven't yet committed to using only 100% cotton in your quilt making, at least plan to commit to it for appliqué. The cotton fabric is so much easier to manipulate than a cotton-poly blend. Polyester has a mind of its own and it is NOT thinking "cooperation!" Unless you purchase your fabric in a quilting supply store, you will really need to pay attention to your purchase. The big chains often mix the cotton-poly blends in with the cotton and it is hard to tell the difference.

If you have a mystery fabric at home and you want to test for the content, cut a small piece and light a match to it. If the fabric burns and becomes ash, you have 100% cotton. A cotton-poly blend will yield ash and little pellets. The pellets will be the melted polyester content.

Thread

There are two schools of thought on thread; cotton thread vs. silk thread for appliqué. The two have points in common but are diametrically opposed.

Both groups agree that thinner threads hide the best. The finer 60-weight cotton is a good choice for appliqué. The 50-weight cotton thread, more commonly used for machine piecing, won't go through the eye of my #11 needle.

Some quilters insist one should only use cotton thread on cotton fabrics and other quilters really like the feel of 50-weight silk thread. It glides so easily through the fabric and also hides.

Both groups agree the thread color should match the appliqué fabric, never the background. While there are those who insist on matching the color, there are others who insist matching value is good enough.

I think the most important thing is to match the color of the appliqué fabric. Sometimes, if I just cannot find the right color, I will fall back on matching the value. I may use a charcoal gray instead of the blue I want. I might even use blue for a green. While I do love the feel of silk thread, if I cannot find the right color, I will use cotton.

Needles

Since I don't use a thimble to appliqué (I don't have the needle control with a thimble on my finger) I have found the Straw or Milliners needles are the best for me. They are a little longer than Sharps. The shorter Sharps make a hole in my finger that hurts. The Straw is long enough to pass that tender spot and still afford me the control I want.

That being said, the more important thing, though, is for you to use the correct size needle. Whether you use the Straw or the Sharp, I highly recom-

mend the #11. I really see a difference in the quality of my stitches between the #11 and anything larger, such as a #10. (The numbering system for needles is such that as the number increases, the shaft of the needle will be incrementally smaller.)

Template material

I've tried all sorts of different template systems. I keep going back to that old kitchen staple, freezer paper. Even though I use a sandpaper board under my fabric to keep it from slipping while I trace the template, there is nothing that keeps my template from slipping while I trace, unless, of course, the template is adhered to the fabric. That's what freezer paper does. When I press it with a hot, dry iron (I use the wool setting) the shiny side against the right side of the fabric, the template stays where I want it to until I release it by passing a pin between the paper and the fabric.

Marking

The marking I do is to define my turn-under line for the seam allowance. Once the template is adhered to the appliqué fabric, I trace it with a marker. My fabric will determine which marker I use. A dark fabric will require a marker that can be seen. You will find a number of different light markers, including soapstone and chalk. I favor the chalk, but please experiment and discover what you like. Just remember a dark fabric requires a light marker, and a light fabric requires a dark marker.

Since the line you draw is in the seam allowance, it really doesn't matter how thin you make your line. As long as you are sure to turn that line all the way under, it does not matter if the line is permanent or will come out in washing. I do suggest if you decide to use a permanent marker as some appliqué artists do, you test the fabric to make sure the marks won't shadow through a thinner fabric.

Scissors

You will need both paper scissors and fabric scissors. The paper scissors will be used to cut your freezer paper templates. The fabric scissors will be used to trim your seam allowances. Either can be used to clip thread.

Since you will be working with small pieces, whether they are the templates or the appliqué fabric pieces, I recommend you use small scissors. I use 4" embroidery scissors for my fabric. I also have a pair of very sharp 4" utility scissors for my templates. For clipping in my seam allowances, I need the scissor blades to be very sharp all the way to the very sharp points.

Pins

There are plenty of methods for attaching the appliqué piece to the background while you stitch. I prefer to pin baste. It is important to note; I use small pins! There are 3/4" appliqué pins and 1/2" sequin pins that are small. Unfortunately I can't seem to manage the 1/2" pins so I use the 3/4" pins. You need to try the ones that work best

for you. However, it is important to note that pins that are any longer than 3/4" are too long. Your thread will get tangled on the longer pins. If you insist on using them, however, pin from the back of your block.

Preparation

Begin by tracing the appliqué pattern on the non-shiny side of the freezer paper. Be sure to include the numbers. The numbers are the stitching sequence. Stitching is from the background forward so the design element that is closest to you is the last one to be stitched.

I recommend you cut the templates at the ironing board. As you audition your fabrics for your design, you will find it easier to visualize if you cut the templates as you choose the fabric. If you cut the templates apart and then try to choose the fabrics, you won't be able to tell to what part of the design the shapes correspond. In addition, if you want to "fussy cut" something you'll find orienting the shape on the fabric is easier.

When placing the templates on the right side of the appliqué fabric, orient them so as many of the edges as possible are on the bias of the fabric. It is much easier to work with shapes, turning under the seam allowances, which are on the bias than on the straight of grain. Remember, the shiny side of the freezer paper is placed down on the right side of the fabric. With your iron set on the wool setting, press the freezer paper with a dry iron. If your iron runs cool, increase the setting to "cotton." If the freezer paper doesn't stay adhered to the fabric, the iron needs to be hotter.

Place the fabric, with the template adhered, onto a sandpaper board, or a piece of fine sandpaper that you glue to a piece of cardboard, wood or a manila folder. As you trace the template, the sandpaper will grip the fabric and keep it from shifting.

Trace the template with the marker that is appropriate for your fabric. I recommend you trace over the top of the template edge so the marker doesn't lift the freezer paper. By this I mean the template should be between the tip of your marker and your hand.

Once all of the templates are traced, trim your seam allowances to 3/16 of an inch and then stack the pieces in numerical order with #1 on top.

Placement Overlay

Some appliqué artists trace the pattern onto their background fabric. I don't because I know I run the risk of not covering the lines with the appliqué. Instead, I trace my design onto a piece of clear upholstery vinyl or a clear report page protector, making sure I include the center and side-center markings. I use the overlay as a guide for placing my appliqué pieces. The page protector will serve as an overlay as well as a pocket to hold my prepared appliqué pieces as I work.

You'll find the vinyl at most hobby supply stores or most fabric centers that also carry home decoration fabrics. Inspect it carefully before purchasing. If the vinyl wants to stretch or is rippled from

stretching, I think it's too thin. The really heavy vinyl is difficult to pin through and costs quite a bit. I use the middle one. Page protectors are easily found in office supply stores.

Trace the pattern onto the vinyl with a permanent marker. I favor the fine point Sharpie from Sanford. For some reason the ink in the ultra fine point wants to bead up on me, but other quilters like it better. Experiment a bit and find the one you like best.

If you are tracing a symmetrical design onto the vinyl, be sure to mark something on the vinyl such as the name of the block so you'll always know which is the side you marked. I don't recommend a "T" at the top edge, though, for obvious reasons.

Be sure to save the tissue that comes with the vinyl. While the permanent marking pen won't rub off, the marks will transfer if the vinyl surface touches vinyl. Place the tissue on the side you mark before rolling or folding for storing.

Background preparation

Because your appliqué stitches can distort the background square and because handling the fabric while stitching can fray the edges, I recommend you cut your background fabric one or two inches larger than needed. A 12-inch finished block would first be cut 13 1/2 or 14 1/2 inches square. (In the case of the Horn of Plenty blocks, you'll cut your blocks 10 1/2" x 13 1/2.") Once you complete all of the appliqué, you will trim the block down to the size you need, squaring the edges and eliminating any fraying. If somehow your design did not end up in the center as you had planned, trimming will fix that, too.

Begin by folding the background block in half and creasing the fold. I just finger press because an iron very often sets those creases for good. Open the block, turn it a quarter turn and fold in half again, carefully aligning the first fold. Finger press the crease. Remember, the edges will be trimmed, so it won't matter if the edges don't match. It is important, however, for the folds to be perfectly perpendicular. If you fold the block in half and then in half again, you run the risk of the two creases not being perpendicular. Even though it may seem easier, you'll do a better job if you crease in both directions independently. The creases will be matched to the center and side-center markings on the placement overlay.

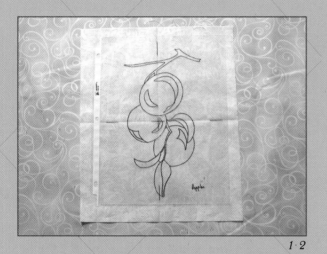

1·2

Place your block background on a flat surface. You may be more comfortable working at a table. I actually use my sandpaper board on my lap as a table while I sit in my easy chair with my feet up. Place the placement overlay on top, aligning the center and side-center markings with the creases in your fabric. (1-2)

If you think you need an extra hand, pin the overlay in three places. If you're right-handed you'll want to pin on the left side. Left-handers will pin on the right.

With the freezer paper still attached to the appliqué piece, slip the shape between the fabric and the vinyl. When the lines on the overlay and the edge of the freezer paper template are perfectly lined up, gently pull the overlay back and place two or three pins in the seam allowance to secure the appliqué piece.

Remove the freezer paper by slipping a pin between the fabric and the freezer paper. Remember, the freezer paper is on the bias of the fabric. Just pulling the paper off will stretch the shape.

Move the pins to the inside of the shape within the turn-under lines. Place the pins parallel to the lines and no closer than 1/4" from the line. Pin in the direction you'll be stitching. Right-handed quilters should stitch from right to left or counter-clockwise around the appliqué. Left-handed quilters should stitch from left to right or clockwise around the appliqué.

Pin baste just one piece at a time, stitch it to the background, then add the next piece.

Threading the needle

The most important thing you need to remember is you need to knot the correct end of the thread. Thread has a twist that will cause problems for you as you draw the thread through the fabric if you draw it "backwards." As you pull an 18-inch piece of thread from the spool, remember you will knot the end you cut. Now, that said, if you transfer the thread to a bobbin as some quilters do to economize on space, notice that you are changing the direction of the twist. In that case, you will need to knot the opposite end.

Cut your thread on an angle and it will be easier to pass the thread through the eye of the needle. Did you know there's a front door and back door to a needle? The way the eye is punched into the needle causes a concave area around the eye. That's the front door. So if you're having trouble, turn the needle over and try again.

The knot you make is easy. Place your needle between your thumb and forefinger. Place the end of the thread, the end to be knotted, cross-wise over the needle and hold it, too, between your thumb and forefinger. (1-3a) Wrap the same end of the thread around the needle 2-4 times; remember you're still holding the very end. Slide the wrapping between your thumb and forefinger. With your other hand, draw the needle through your finger and thumb (and the thread wraps) and continue to pull until you have reached the end and the thread is knotted. (1-3b) Think of this as nothing more than a French knot that isn't attached to anything.

1-3a

1-3b

The Appliqué Stitch

The first thing to consider is where to begin stitching. Never begin on a corner, inside or outside, sharp or curved, unless that corner is overlapped by another appliqué shape. If no part of the shape will be overlapped by another shape, then I try to begin on a relatively straight area. Naturally, a circle has no straight area, so I just begin anywhere.

Begin by bringing the needle through the appliqué piece on the turn-under line from the back to the right side. I never make knots on the back of my appliqué block. The tail of the knot may very well shadow through the background fabric, especially if the background fabric is very light. Bury it in the fold of the seam allowance.

With the tip of your needle, turn the seam allowance under the appliqué shape until the line totally disappears. Turn under just enough for your thumbnail to hold in place. Put the tip of the needle into the background barely under the fold but right where the thread is coming from the fold. (1-4) Travel forward two or three threads and come up into the appliqué and draw your needle out in the fold. Coming out on top will let your stitches show, as the thread will be wrapping around the edge. Pull the thread snug but not so tight it draws the appliqué and makes a pucker. Repeat, making sure your needle goes into the background just barely under the fold where the thread is coming. As you pull the thread you will notice the stitch disappears. Placing the needle into the background next to the appliqué will cause your stitches to appear as little thorns around the appliqué.

Since I don't want knots on the back of my block, I end by taking a last stitch and then stitching a stitch backward and then taking the stitch forward again. This makes a figure eight and locks the thread. I bury the thread in the appliqué between the background and appliqué about an inch, and cut the excess away.

1-4

Towels made by Susan Winnie, Overland Park, KS 2004.

CHAPTER TWO –
Block Techniques

As I completed the appliqué work on my "Horn of Plenty" quilt, I realized the quilt deserved to be hand quilted. I also knew I, notorious for being VERY slow with my hand quilting skills, would never be able to get the quilt finished in time to be included in this book unless I had help.

I knew several members of a group of quilters who meet every Wednesday to participate in an old fashioned quilting bee. These ladies get together every week around a quilting frame to share in friendship, support each other in times of joy and challenge and earn funds for the Legler Barn Museum in Lenexa, Kansas. In fact, the bee takes place in the reconstructed stone barn and becomes one of the exhibits that visitors to the museum are lucky to see in action - a living history that continues.

The Legler Barn Quilters began meeting in 1987. At the time there were just four members. Over the years the group has grown and fluctuated. As of this writing, there are 16 dedicated members of all ages, backgrounds and nationalities. Their purpose has been two-fold. The quilters raise money for the Legler Barn Museum with their quilting and encourage the art of hand quilting. The stone-built Legler Barn, originally located at 95th and Quivira on the southern edge of Lenexa, Kansas, was the livestock barn on the property of Swiss immigrants Adam and Elisabeth Legler. Originally built in 1864, the barn was disassembled stone by stone in 1972 and moved to its new

home on 87th Street at Lackman in Lenexa and reassembled like a giant 3-dimensional puzzle. The Barn opened as a museum in 1983.

Legler Barn; Courtesy of Lenexa Historical Society

Over the years, the Legler Barn Quilters have quilted a number of quilts for each other, other quilters, non-quilters and a special quilt that is exhibited every fall at Lenexa's Spinach Festival. A drawing is held and some lucky person is the recipient of The Barn Quilters' fine work.

I am absolutely delighted this loving group of women invited me into their midst. I've made new friends and am blessed with the opportunity to know how it feels to belong to a group of caring, giving and supportive women over the quilting frame! (2-2, 2-3)

left to right: Ann Piette, Pat White, Elaine Pegram, Phillys Bartels, C.J. Cook, Mary Strege, Jean Aarnold , Mary Feagins   2-2

back row left to right: Lang Davis, Wava Stoker, front row left to right: Linda Mooney, Kathy Delaney, Jeanne Poore   2-3

TECHNIQUES USED IN COMPLETING THE BLOCKS

Piecing the appliqué

While appliquéing each individual piece to the background is a valid method of appliqué, I actually like to piece appliqué units together before applying them to the background whenever possible. I call this piecing my appliqué. I find it easy to work this way and it allows me to cut the background out from behind the appliqué before quilting so I only have to stitch through the single layer of the top, the batting and the backing.

Layering the appliqué on the background means more than one layer of fabric in the top to try to quilt through. I get more consistent stitches when I can eliminate bulk.

As I prepare my appliqué shapes, I plan ahead. I treat one shape as the background to the previous shape when it is part of a unit. For instance, take a look at the two-leaf unit illustrated below. If I let #3 act as background to #4, and #2 act as background to #4, I can piece this unit before applying the two leaves as one to my background.

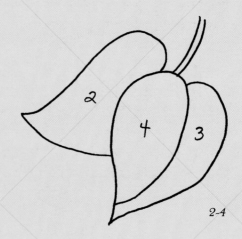

2-4

Adhere the freezer paper templates to the appliqué fabric and trace with the appropriate marker. Cut 3/16" seam allowances on the edges that will be appliquéd directly to the background only. The edge of #4 that meets #3 gets appliquéd to #3. Leave about 3/4" to an inch of extra fabric for seam allowance on #3. This will give you places to pin baste while you stitch. Once the seam is stitched, trim the excess away from underneath. Leave an excess of 3/4" to an inch on the edge of piece #2 that meets the edge of #4. The excess gives you a place to pin baste while you stitch. Again, once you have stitched the #4 to #2 you can trim the seam allowance to 3/16".

When appliquéing the unit to the background, begin by stitching #2. Remember, we always stitch the piece "farthest away" first and since #2 leaf is actually behind #3/4 leaf, it is farthest.

Cut-away appliqué

Let's face it. The stems on most of these blocks are really thin! Don't let that scare you! They only seem complicated because the idea of such a small piece of fabric seems hard to handle. So don't!

Adhere your freezer paper template to the right side of the fabric, making sure as many edges as possible are on the bias, and trace the template with the proper marking tool. Do not cut seam allowance; instead, cut the fabric all around about a half an inch away from the drawn line. This will give you places to pin baste while you stitch. (2-5) Using your overlay to position your appliqué piece, place the shape before removing the freezer paper. The template really makes it much easier to move the fabric shape into place. Place your pins in the excess fabric opposite of the edge you will be stitching. That is, if you will be stitching the right side of a stem, place the pins in the excess on the left side of the stem. Again, pin in the direction you'll be stitching so you don't knock the pins out with your knuckles.

With your small scissors, cut the seam allowance about two inches ahead of your stitching. Depending on the width of the stem, you may have to cut a seam allowance that is narrower than the 3/16" that I recommended earlier. Because the seam allowance will be narrow, pay attention to the weave of your fabric. A looser woven fabric may not work as well for this technique. Turning the seam allowance with the point of your needle could fray it. I tend to use batik fabrics for my stems, as I know the weave is very tight. By the way, because batik fabrics are so closely woven, I never use a needle any larger than a #11.

2-5

Begin turning under the seam allowance and stitch. As you approach the end of the first two inches, cut more seam allowance. Just cut a couple of inches at a time. This keeps the shape in place and you don't run the risk of it shifting out of place.

If I have a simple short stem, I often go ahead and cut the seam allowance for one side of the stem, leaving the other side with extra fabric for my pins. After stitching the first side, I cut the seam allowance for the second side and stitch.

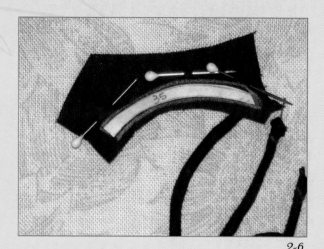

2-6

The Twist

There are two occasions where I will use a technique I call "the twist." (The name refers to what I do with the seam allowance so I can have the seam allowance going in both directions on the one seam.)

Twist #1: If I have a seam that is overlapped on one end and is overlapping another piece on the other end, I will twist the seam allowance so I don't have to create any outside points. The overlapping will create the point.

Twist #2: If I have a seam that is overlapped on both ends by another piece, yet I want the shape that is underneath to appear as if it is on top, I will twist the seam allowance on both ends so the middle seems to be on top. Even though appliqué is flat, the direction of the seam allowances will give the illusion of dimension.

Twist #1

An example of Twist #1, the most common twist I employ, is in the Apricot block. (2-7) I denote a seam for a twist with a slash mark across the seam and arrows on either side of the slash mark. The slash mark indicates where to clip the seam allowance. My arrows indicate which appliqué shape is on top. Obviously, both of the appliqué pieces that share a seam cannot be on the top! To accomplish it, the seam allowance must be split and pressed in opposite directions.

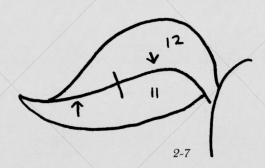

2-7

Begin by tracing the template on the fabric as you do usually. Without removing the freezer paper template, clip the seam allowance where the slash mark is on the template. Clip right up to the template. Repeat with the corresponding appliqué piece. The clips should match exactly, so it is important that you include the slash mark across the seam line as you trace the pattern onto your freezer paper. Include the arrows so you remember which shape is on top when you are stitching.

Fit the two appliqué shapes together in the slash, making sure your arrows are on top. (2-8) There won't be much space to pin baste, so you may find it easier to just hold the two shapes together as you stitch.

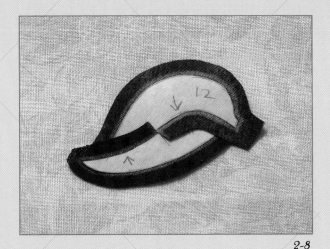

2-8

Begin stitching at the slash and stitch out to the end. Bury your thread and begin again at the slash and stitch to the other end. Your slash point will not show if you have turned under the seam allowance so the tracing line totally disappears. (2-9) Left handers will stitch from the end toward the center.

Twist #2

An example of Twist #2 occurs in the Apple block. Piece #5 represents the bottom side of the leaf as it curls up over the top of the leaf represented by piece #6. In order for the edge of the leaf to look like it is on top, you would

have to appliqué by turning the corners, unless you can overlap those points by piece #6. To do so, you make two twists on the same seam. (2-10a)

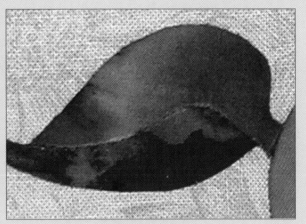

2-9

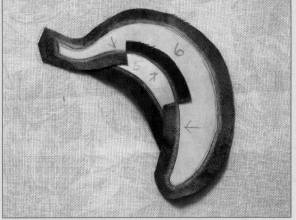

2-10a

2-10b

The double twist works the same way, except you work from one clip out to the end and then the other clip out to the other end. Stitch the seam between the two clips last, being sure to turn under the seam allowance completely so the tracing line doesn't show and no little "fuzzies" try to escape at the clips. (2-10b) Left handers work from the outside edge in toward the center.

On rare occasions you may run across a situation where you will be piecing the appliqué and working a twist at the same time. Remember, piecing the appliqué leaves excess fabric before stitching, followed by trimming the seam allowance after stitching. The twist, while it is actually piecing the appliqué, does not allow excess fabric before stitching.

On the Pomegranate block you will find just such an instance. Pieces #19 and #20 employ both techniques. Below is an illustration that will show you how I cut shape #19. Notice that I cut the seam allowance on the side that gets the twist but left excess on the other side.

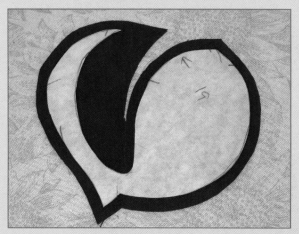

2-11

Circles

Circles can be tedious if you start counting them before you stitch. If you just stitch you won't think there are nearly as many as there are. I recommend that you don't count! I employ two different methods for making my circles, depending on their size.

Free-hand ~ less than 1/2" in diameter

The first secret to stitching circles free-hand is to turn under just enough seam allowance to take one stitch at a time. If you try to turn under too much ahead of your stitching, your edge will not be smooth. (2-12)

The second secret to free-hand circles is to take very small stitches. If you have noticed circles that seem to be jagged along the edge, looking closely will probably reveal longer stitches.

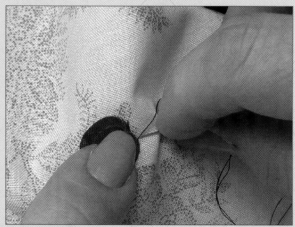

2-12

Short stitches that are close together will result in a smooth curve.

The third secret to free-hand circles is the turn-under line. I have found that tracing the circle line using a drafting tool called a Circle Template results in a better circle. (2-13) Trying to cut a freezer paper template can be very difficult. Tracing around a circular shape and cutting with scissors will very likely distort the circle. The Circle Template is a round "hole" that you trace from the inside. I trace directly onto the right side of my fabric. Then I cut a scant 3/16" seam allowance and stitch, taking small stitches close together and only turning enough ahead to be able to make the one, possibly two, stitches.

I make my circles free-hand only if the circle is less than 1/2" in diameter.

Template form

If I have a larger circle than 1/2", I like to make a form on which to shape my circle. The form requires more fabric on the back to begin and anything less than 1/2" is too small for this.

There are a variety of materials you may use for your form. If you use round stickers from the office supply store, you will be limited to the size of the stickers. I'd rather have the flexibility of making my own forms to any size I need. I use sandpaper or heat resistant Mylar plastic template material. There are benefits to each.

If you use sandpaper, begin by tracing a circle, using the Circle Template, on the paper side of the sandpaper. With craft scissors, cut the circle on the outside of the line. The outside of the line is actually the most accurate as the pencil or pen is consistently against the template. The inside of the line can vary depending on the type of pencil you use to trace. Use your very best cutting skills and be sure to turn the paper, as you cut, not the scissors. If you find your circle isn't quite as smooth as you would like, you can use the excess sandpaper to "sand" the edge smooth.

If you use the Mylar template plastic, you can use a circle cutter to cut the template without marking and without scissors. Again, if you need to smooth out an edge, an emery board works well.

You will need a piece of fabric about an inch larger than your circle. If you are using the sandpaper form, you will be able to hold the sandpaper side of the form against the wrong side of the fabric and it won't slip. If you use the Mylar, trace the form lightly on the wrong side of the fabric.

I suggest you use a strong thread for the next step. I use hand-quilting thread and I don't worry about the color. I also use a sturdier needle than my favorite #11 Straw.

You will be stitching a running stitch around the circle about 1/8" from the edge of the form or the traced line, on the outside of the circle. Take long stitches and short stitches. The long stitch should be on the wrong side of the fabric while the short stitches are on the right side of the fabric. (2-15) Finish by bringing your needle through the fabric to the right side of the fabric.

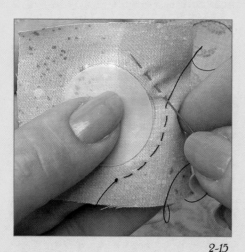

2-15

Trim away the excess fabric about 3/16" from the stitching. If you cut too close, you will find that the fabric will disintegrate in the next step.

Put the form back against the wrong side of the fabric, inside the running stitch, and pull the thread, drawing the fabric tightly around the form. Pull the thread across the body of the circle, not away from it. Hold the thread tight and distribute the gathers so you have no pleats on the edge of the circle. When satisfied and still holding the thread very taut, knot the thread right at the fabric. Take a stitch, then take a second stitch without pulling the loop completely. Pass the needle through the loop twice and then pull for a secure knot.

Press the circle with a steam iron. For a really sharp crease on the edge, cover the circle immediately with a wooden clapper. (2-16) This is a tool used in tailoring. If you don't have one, you can just use a clean, unfinished piece of smooth wood. Turn the circle over, press again with a steam iron and hit it again with the clapper. The wood will absorb the heat and the moisture and set the crease.

2-16

I make a form for each circle I will be stitching. I also leave the form inside the circle until I am ready to stitch the circle to my block. Keep the forms for another project.

When ready to stitch the circle to your block, clip the excess fabric from the wrong side of the circle so you are left with just a 3/16" seam allowance. You can cut away all of the running stitch or just enough to be able to slip the form out of the circle. Use your placement overlay to place the circle on your block. I use, at most, just three pins to baste the circle in place and then I remove one to begin stitching. So, I'm really only using two pins! (2-17) I recommend that you appliqué the circle to the background with small stitches.

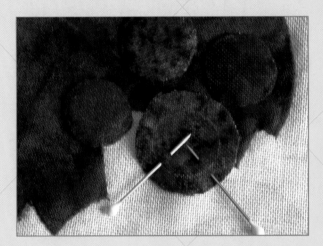

2-17

Reverse Appliqué

On the Loganberry block you will notice some very small appliqué shapes. Conventional appliqué would be very difficult with such small pieces! I used a technique called "reverse" appliqué to make those tiny shapes. Instead of adding a shape to the appliqué, I open a slit and turn under a very tiny seam allowance to reveal the fabric underneath, thus reverse. Remember,

for this scant seam allowance, you really must stitch with very small and close stitches.

2-18

I suggest you consider the weave of your fabric for this particular block. A loose weave will not work as well since the seam allowance is so narrow. I often use batik fabric, which has a very tight weave.

Combining shapes

You will find some instances where a shape is separated by another shape, such as when one branch crosses another branch. I have numbered the two parts of the one shape on the pattern with two numbers for clarity. When I stitched my blocks, however, I combined the shapes and made them one.

Take a look at the Pear block. Appliqué pieces #1 and #2 are the same stem. Feel free to adhere the two templates onto the fabric together, using the placement overlay for guidance, and then stitching the stem as a whole. I did! (2-19)

I also combined the two parts of piece #3. If you like, you may even wish to combine #4 and #6 into one. If the break between the two parts of a shape is fairly narrow, I will definitely combine the two parts. Be careful, though, that the shape underneath does not shadow through the shape on top. In that case, you just want to make it the two separate shapes.

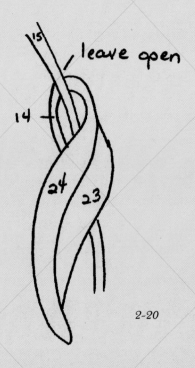

2-20

2-19

"Leave Open" notes

Sometimes you will find that a shape will be on top of a shape and under it at the same time. (2-20) On the Orange block you will find just such an instance. The stem of the orange will be on top of the branch and under it at the same time. When that happens I will leave open part of the seam so I can go back later and slip the piece under the edge. I close the open seam after I have stitched the new shape.

CHAPTER THREE
The Horn of Plenty Quilt

On the following pages you will find the block patterns for Eveline Foland's "Horn of Plenty." I have included the patterns as they appeared in The Kansas City Star in 1932, as well as Ms. Foland's notes regarding color choices. Following that, you will find a photograph of my rendition and my redrawn patterns of the blocks. If there are any techniques I find helpful, I list those as well. Following the blocks, you will find instructions for completing your quilt, including information about binding a quilt with a scalloped edge. I hope you enjoy recreating Eveline Foland's wonderful quilt!

The Horn of Plenty quilt consists of 18 appliquéd blocks and 17 alternate blocks with the Horn of Plenty quilting design. I made my quilt with just one background fabric for both blocks and border, but you may want to use a different fabric for your border. The quilt also has no sashing, but you may want to include it to make the quilt larger.

The one change I made to Eveline Foland's layout was to make five rows of seven blocks making a square quilt instead of the rectangle Ms. Foland's design resulted in.

I have figured in extra fabric for blocks in case you make a mistake in cutting. I'd rather have 3/8 of a yard left over than to run short because I cut wrong! I've added an extra 1/4 yard for cutting mistakes in the scallop fabric.

While I used hand dyed fabric, batik fabrics and contemporary prints for my appliqué, I tried to follow Eveline Foland's suggestions for color wherever I could.

Fabric requirements: for a quilt that is 83" x 80"

• 3 3/4 yards for block background
• 2 1/2 yards for the mitered border
• 2 yards for the border swags
• 1 1/2 yards for bias binding (5/8 yard if you make a straight edge instead of scallops)
• Assorted fabrics for the appliqué — if you don't have much of a stash, you might begin by collecting fat quarters of different greens and 1/8 yard pieces of your fruit colors, including oranges, yellows, reds, purples and blues.
• 4 3/4 yards for backing
• Queen-sized packaged batting

To make the fruit blocks, I began by cutting (5) 13 1/2" strips from the block background fabric. Then I cut each of the strips into (4) 10 1/2"x 13 1/2" rectangles, although I only needed two from the fifth strip. This gave me extra fabric that I could later trim to 9 1/2"x 12 1/2" before I constructed the quilt top.

THE BLOCKS

The apple is
number one
in series.

Eveline Toland

THE APPLE

(The following directions appeared with the original pattern in The Kansas City Star, January 5, 1932.)

The first fruit to roll out of the Horn of Plenty quilt series is the rosy apple, queen of winter fruits. The three apples in (the) design we will number for color direction, 1, 2 and 3, beginning at the top. They should be appliquéd in three shades of red, taking care to use only the yellow reds. The first apple should be in the lightest shade with two highlights, the largest one pink, the smallest one yellow. These highlights should be put in just as you would patch a hole.

The middle apple should be in the middle tone with the highlight the same color red as the first apple. The third apple should be a very dark red with the highlight the same as the second apple. The stems should be brown, the top leaf light green with the part curled over a trifle darker. The two bottom leaves are of the darker green.

Directions:

The design should be appliquéd on fine white muslin or broadcloth. Cut each block 10 by 12 inches. If the white fabric used as a background is fine enough it may be placed over the paper and the pattern traced in the middle of the block. Otherwise, use a carbon paper for tracing. First, trace the pattern in the center of the white block. Second, trace the fruit design on the different colored materials, allowing for seams for each part of the design, fruit, leaf and stem. Third, turn narrow hems and appliqué, following traced patterns on white block. The narrow stems may be embroidered in 6-strand embroidery thread. Appliqué the heavier one. When completed, alternate the completed block with the plain ones that are quilted with (the) horn of plenty design. Use three of the fruit blocks in the first row of the quilt, two in the second, three in the third, and so on.

◆

Techniques I used include:
Piecing the Appliqué
Cutaway Appliqué
The Twist #2

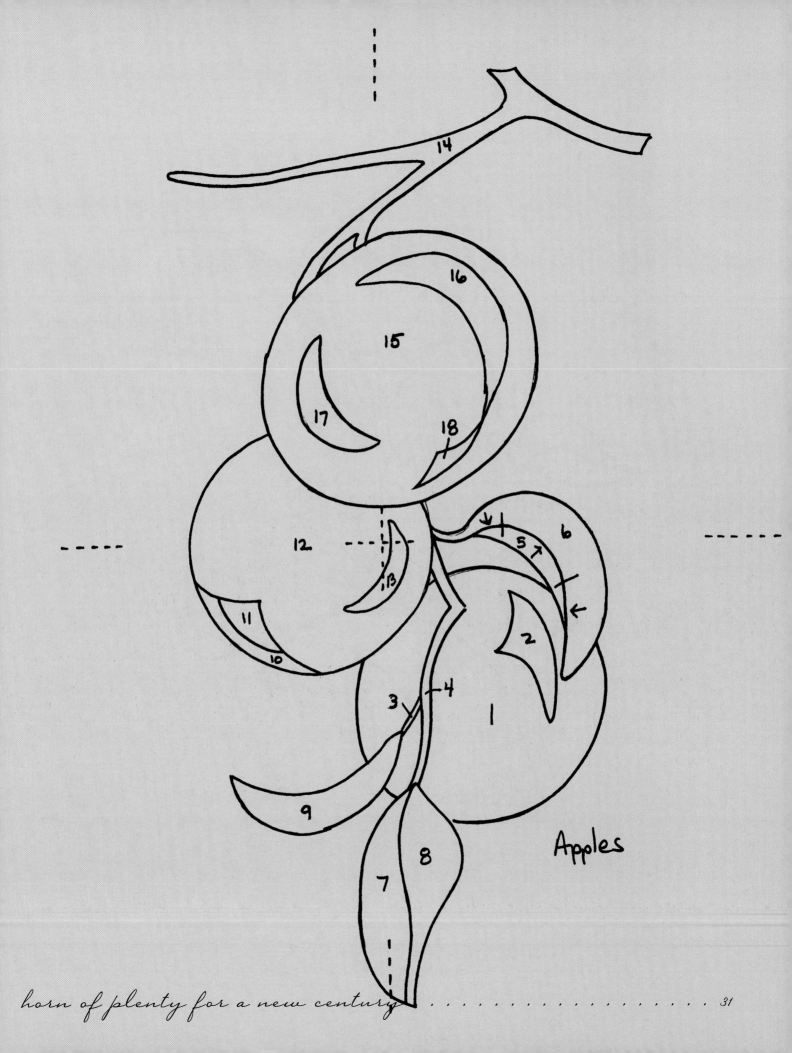

Apples

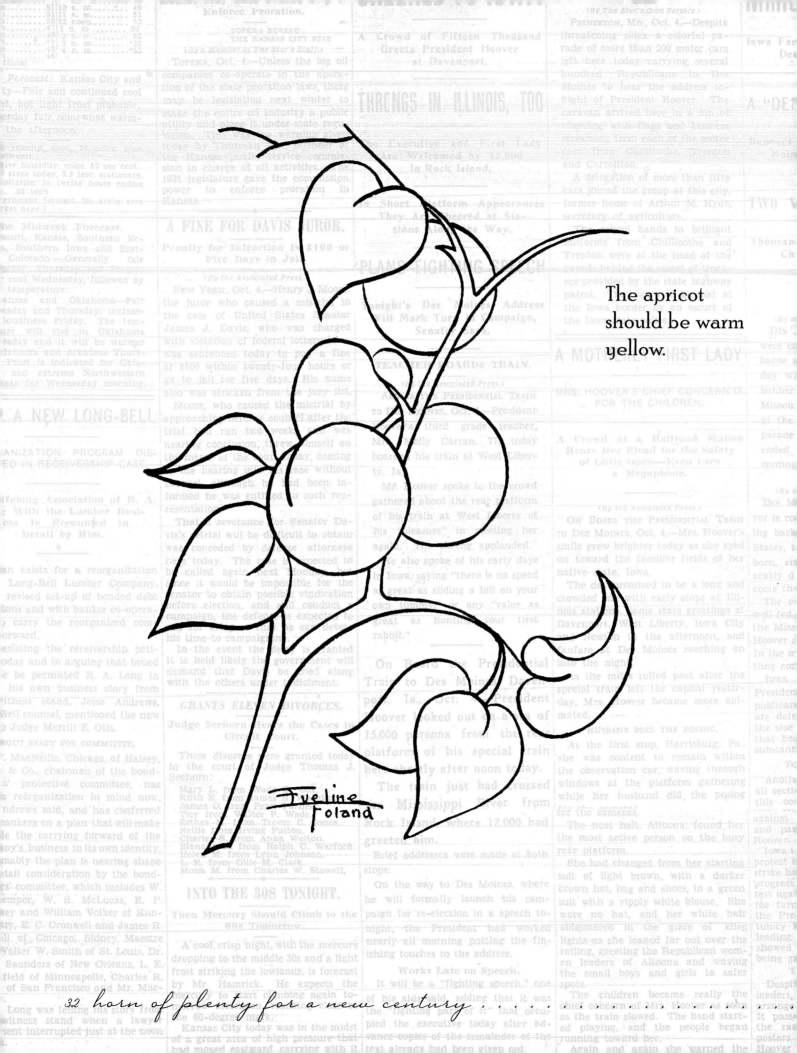

The apricot should be warm yellow.

Eveline Roland

THE APRICOT

*(The following directions appeared with the original pattern
in The Kansas City Star, January 6, 1932.)*

The second in the Horn of Plenty quilt series is the apricot, and
it is really one of the simplest, so far as directions go. The three
apricots should be in their own color a warm yellow. If two
tones can be found it would be interesting to use them for the
two overlapping fruits. The stem should be brown. The leaves
three shades of green, using the darker shade for the back side
of the leaf behind another. Allow for seams.

Techniques I used include:
Piecing the Appliqué
Cutaway Appliqué
The Twist #1

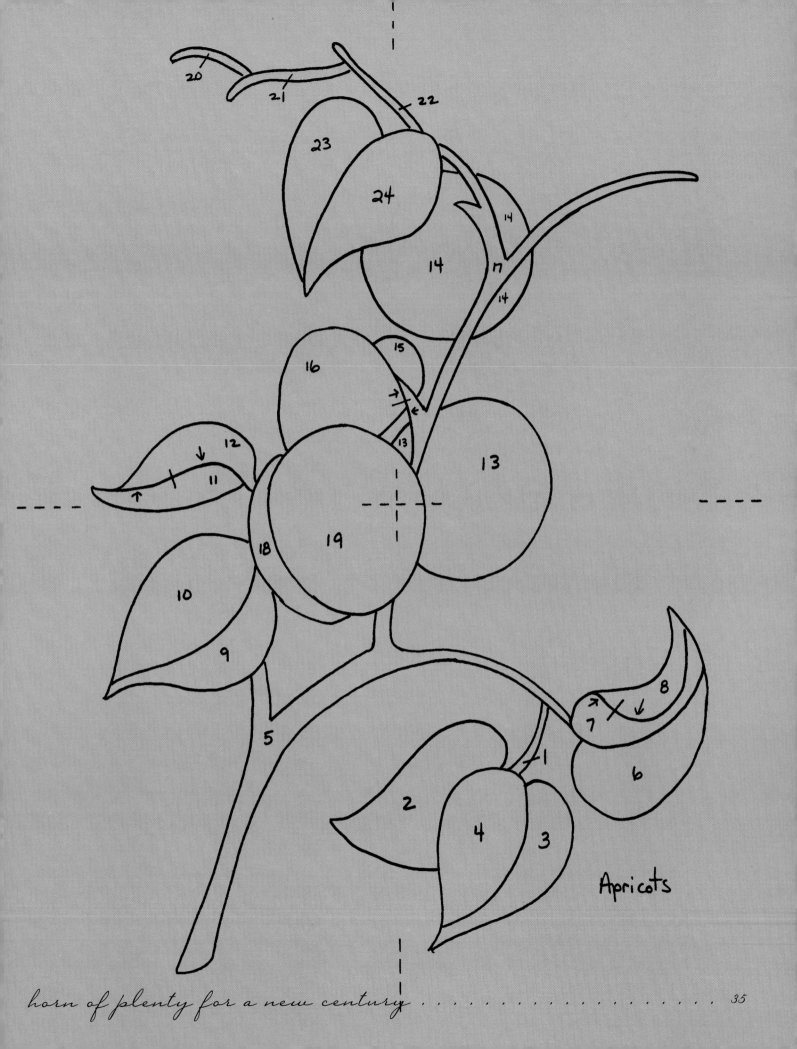

Apricots

The cherry should have its own red.

THE CHERRY

(The following directions appeared with the original pattern

in The Kansas City Star, January 7, 1932.)

The leaves of this spray of cherries, the third in the Horn of Plenty quilt series, should be done in three shades of green — light yellow green, a leaf green and a dark green, which should be used for the under side of the leaf.

The stems should be brown, and the slender stems of the fruit dark green. The cherries should be cherry red, with little black lines showing shadows. Allow for seams.

Techniques I used include:
Piecing the Appliqué
Combining Shapes
Cutaway Appliqué
Template Form Circles
The Twist #1

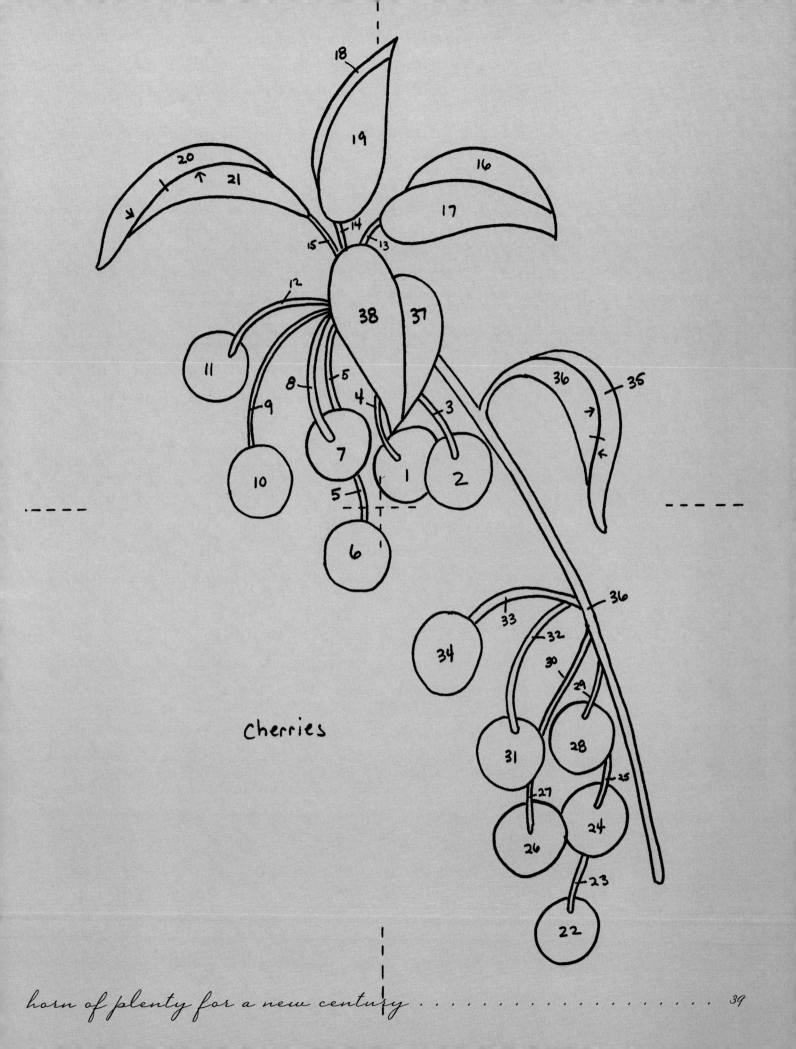

cherries

The blue plum
is the fourth in
the series.

Eveline
Toland

THE BLUE PLUM

(The following directions appeared with the original pattern

in The Kansas City Star, January 8, 1932.)

The large blue plum, the fourth in the Horn of Plenty quilt

series, should be done in deep grape purple, the shade of the

blue plum. The small stems and leaves are green and the wood

is in a leaden shade. Allow for seams.

Techniques I used include:

Piecing the Appliqué

Combining Shapes

Leave open

Cutaway Appliqué

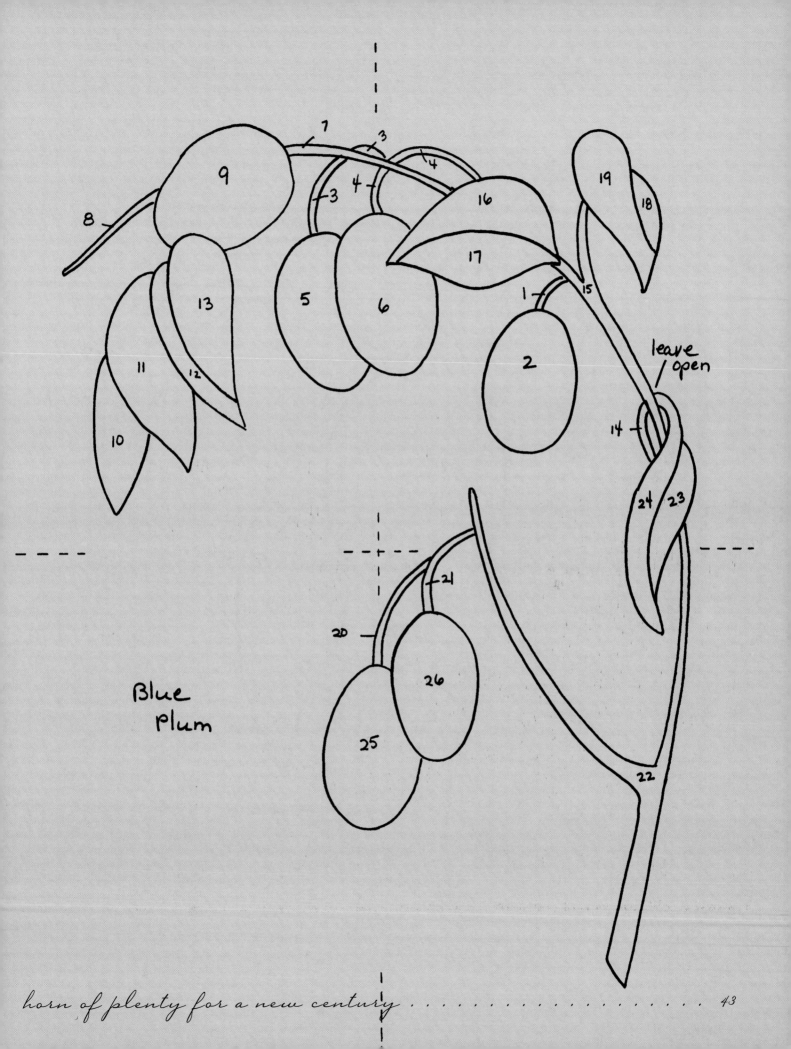

Blue
Plum

The lemon makes a realistic pattern.

THE LEMON

(The following directions appeared with the original pattern

in The Kansas City Star, January 13, 1932.)

The lemon is the (fifth) in the Horn of Plenty quilt series. It is
easy to obtain the perfect shade of yellow for this fruit. The
leaves should be a bright green.

Techniques I used include:
Piecing the Appliqué
Combining Shapes

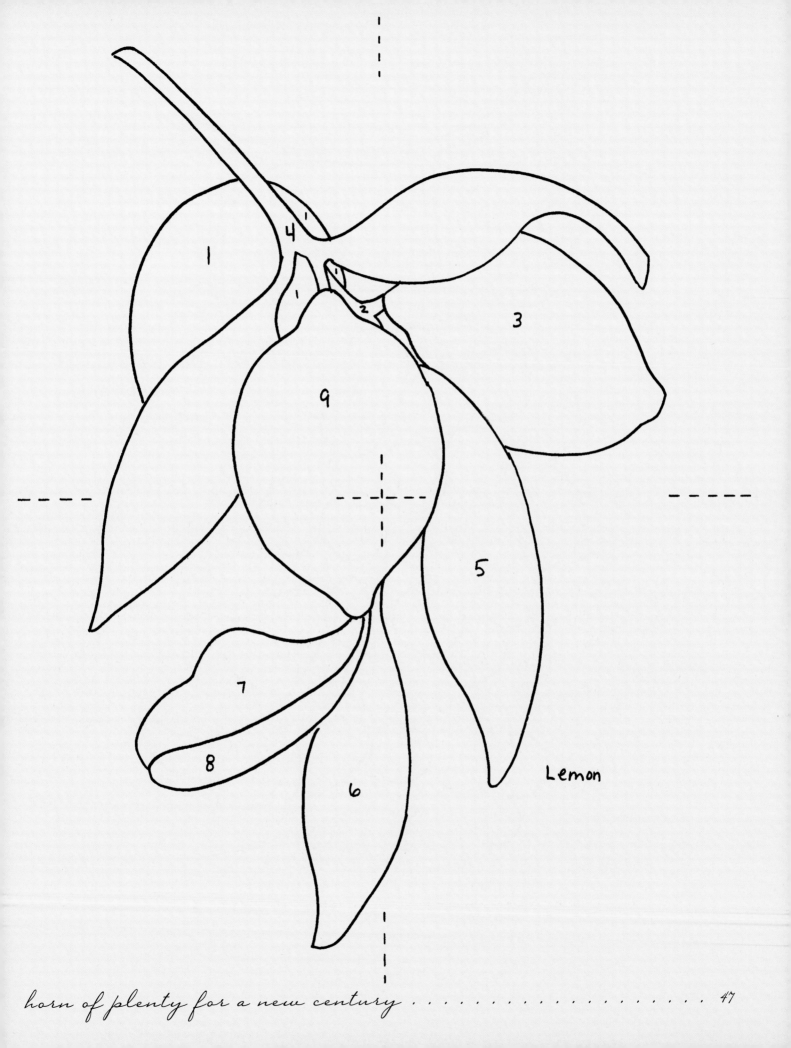

Lemon

The grape should have its own purple.

Eveline
Foland

THE GRAPE

(The following directions appeared with the original pattern

in The Kansas City Star, January 14, 1932.)

The grape is the sixth in the Horn of Plenty quilt series. The stem and leaves should be a dark green. The bunch of grapes are purple, the shade nature paints Concord grapes. The smaller grapes at the top of the bunch may be orchid and lavender to indicate these are not ripe. Allow for seams.

Techniques I used include:
Piecing the Appliqué
Cutaway Appliqué
Template Form Circles

Grape

Select a banana yellow for this block.

Eveline Toland

THE BANANA

(The following directions appeared with the original pattern

in The Kansas City Star, January 15, 1932.)

This is the seventh in the Horn of Plenty quilt series. There are
twenty in all and will appear in The Star as space permits. The
banana is most attractive in its own soft yellow and deep cream
for the inside of the skin. If you make the banana in three
shades of yellow, the middle sections should be a light yellow
and the other sections a deeper shade. This gives a rounded
effect to the fruit. Allow for seams.

◆

Techniques I used include:
Piecing the Appliqué
The Twist #1
Combining Shapes

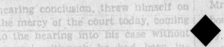

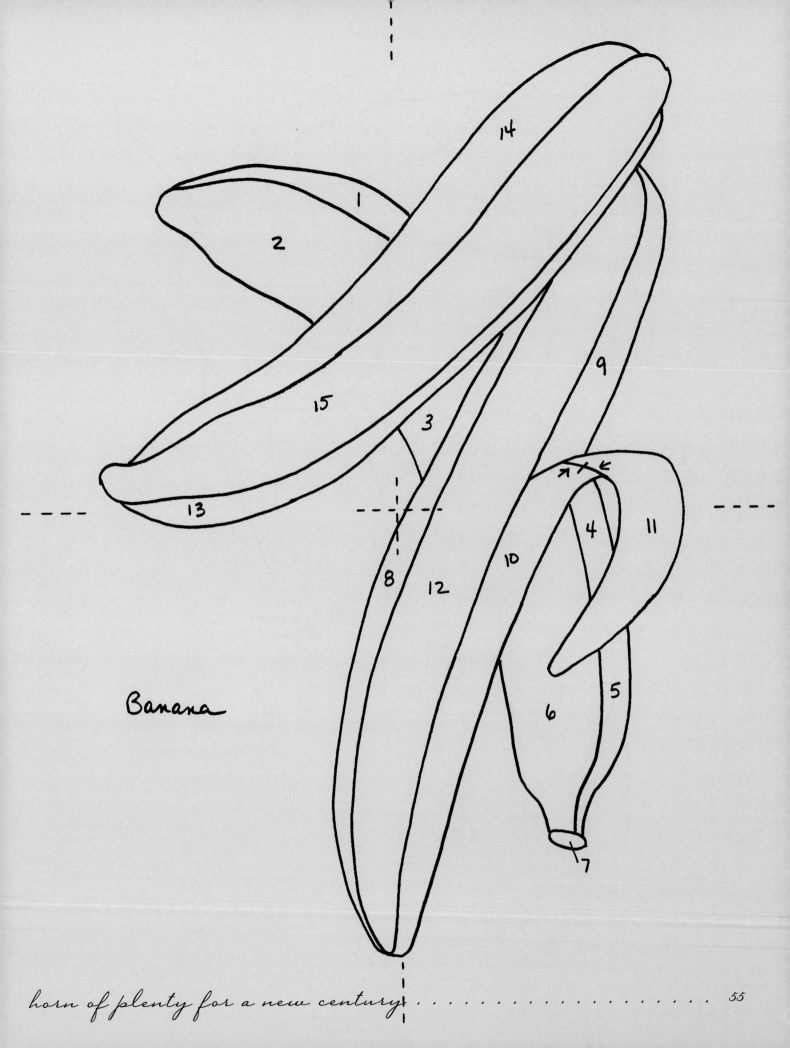

Banana

The peach may be made in fabrics of exact color.

Eveline Toland

THE PEACH

(The following appeared with the original pattern
in The Kansas City Star, January 18, 1932.)

The Quilt Schedule to Date

The Horn of Plenty quilt series now has reached its eighth block. For the use of those who are saving the series it now stands: No. 1, the apple; No. 2, the apricot; No. 3 the cherry; No. 4, the blue plum; No. 5, the lemon; No. 6, the grape; No. 7, the banana; No 8, the peach. Others will follow as space permits. The quilting pattern, The Horn of Plenty, and a leaf design for the border will be included. The last number will be a diagram of the whole quilt with the proper color arrangement of the patterns. The entire series includes twenty-one patterns, eighteen fruit blocks, one quilting design, one border pattern and one diagram. Clip and save, quilters. Use designs for cushions, for decorative motifs for painted furniture, for drawing lessons for the children or any other use an artistic fruit design may fulfill.

This is the eighth of the Horn of Plenty quilt series. The popularity of peach shades will permit this fruit (to be) made in the shades of the natural peach. The fruit may be shaded from deep peach to lighter tones. Allow for seams.

◆

Techniques I used include:
Piecing the Appliqué
Cutaway Appliqué
Leave open

horn of plenty for a new century

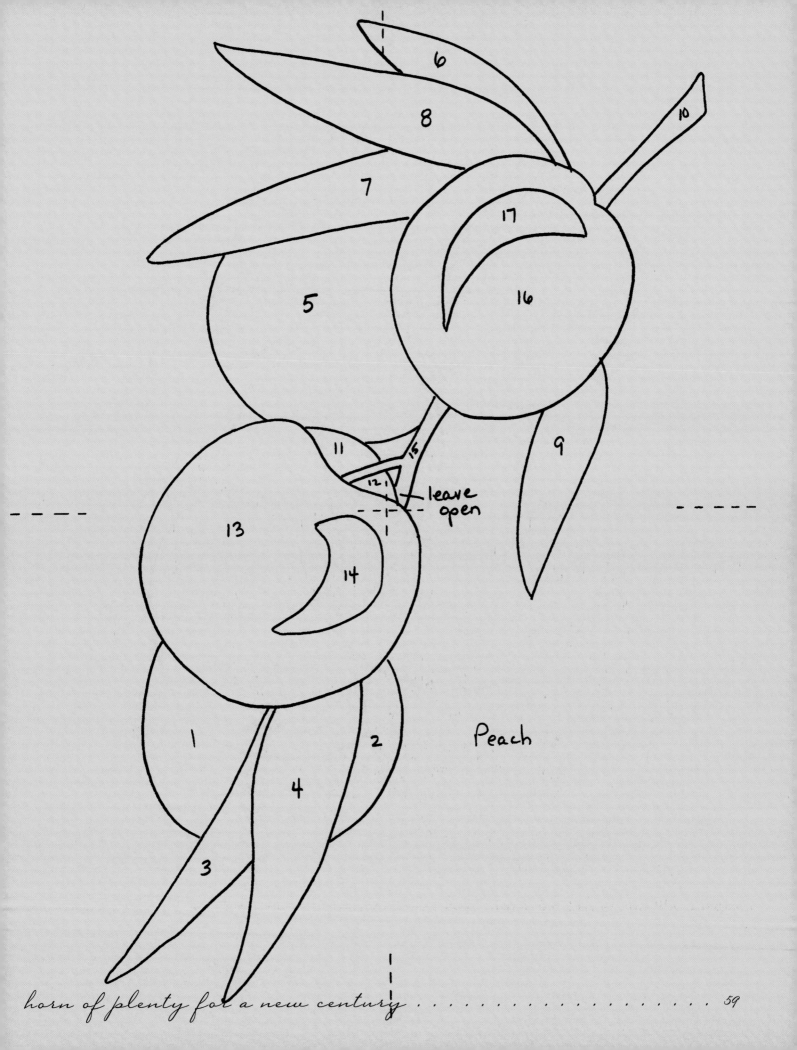

Peach

The orange motif
may be in three
shades.

Eveline
Toland

THE ORANGE

(The following directions appeared with the original pattern

in The Kansas City Star, January 19, 1932.)

The orange is ninth in the Horn of Plenty quilt series. As it is a large spot
of color it may be made in three shades, to indicate the green, the semi-
ripe and the ripe fruit. Allow for seams.

Techniques I used include:
Piecing the Appliqué
Cutaway Appliqué
Leave open
The Twist #1

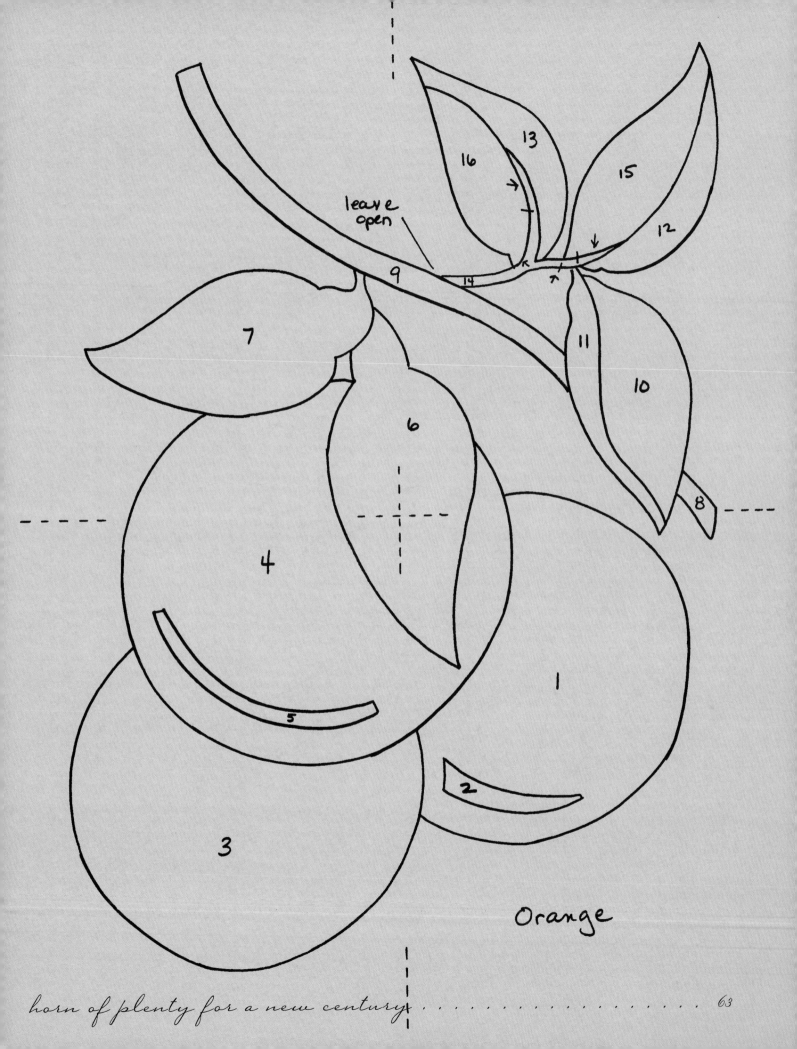

Orange

The pomegranate brings the tropical note.

Eveline Toland

THE POMEGRANATE

(The following directions appeared with the original pattern

in The Kansas City Star, January 21, 1932)

The pomegranate is tenth in the Horn of Plenty quilt series. The fruit, when ripe, is a lovely pink — (see the fruit now in markets). The bottom or spur end of the fruit is olive green. The smaller fruit at the bottom is not quite ripe and should be a soft, grayish pink, with a highlight in the center as indicated. The leaves on the fruit should be embroidered in a darker color. The leaves and stems should be in soft tones of green. Allow for seams.

◆

Techniques I used include:

Cutaway Appliqué

Piecing the Appliqué

The Twist #1

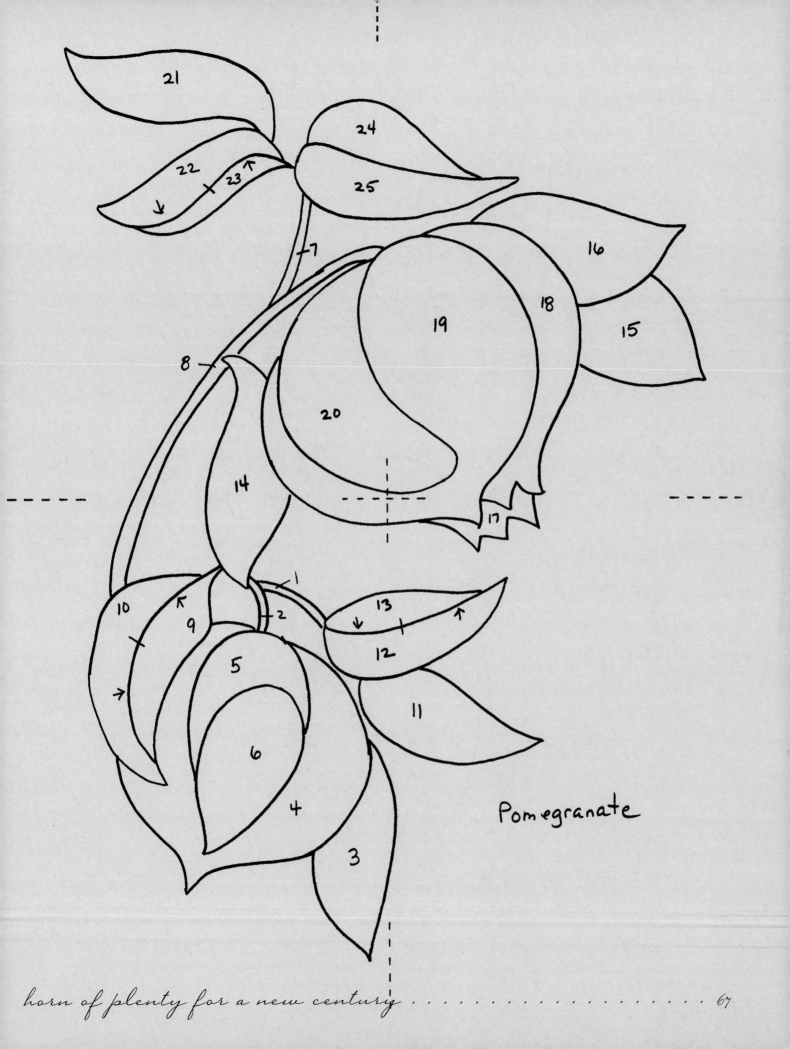

Pomegranate

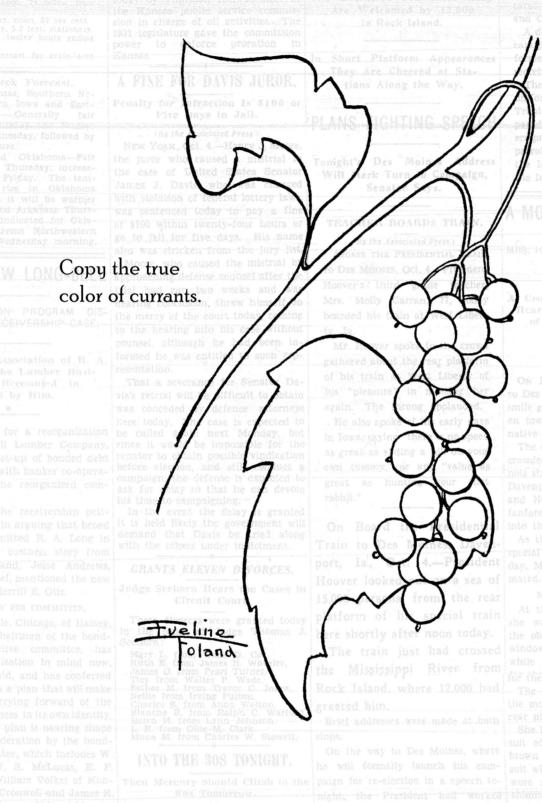

Copy the true
color of currants.

Eveline
Toland

THE CURRANT

*(The following directions appeared with the original pattern
in The Kansas City Star, January 22, 1932.)*

This jolly little bunch of currants is the eleventh in the Horn of Plenty
quilt series. It probably will tax the ingenuity and patience of the
most seasoned quilters, but what an attractive thing it will be when
finished — the stem is wood brown — the stems of the leaves a
lighter green. The top leaf light green, the part rolled over a shade
darker. The bottom leaf darker. The currants should be three shades
of red. Allow for seams.

Techniques I used include:
Cutaway Appliqué
Piecing the Appliqué
"Leave open"
Free-hand Circles

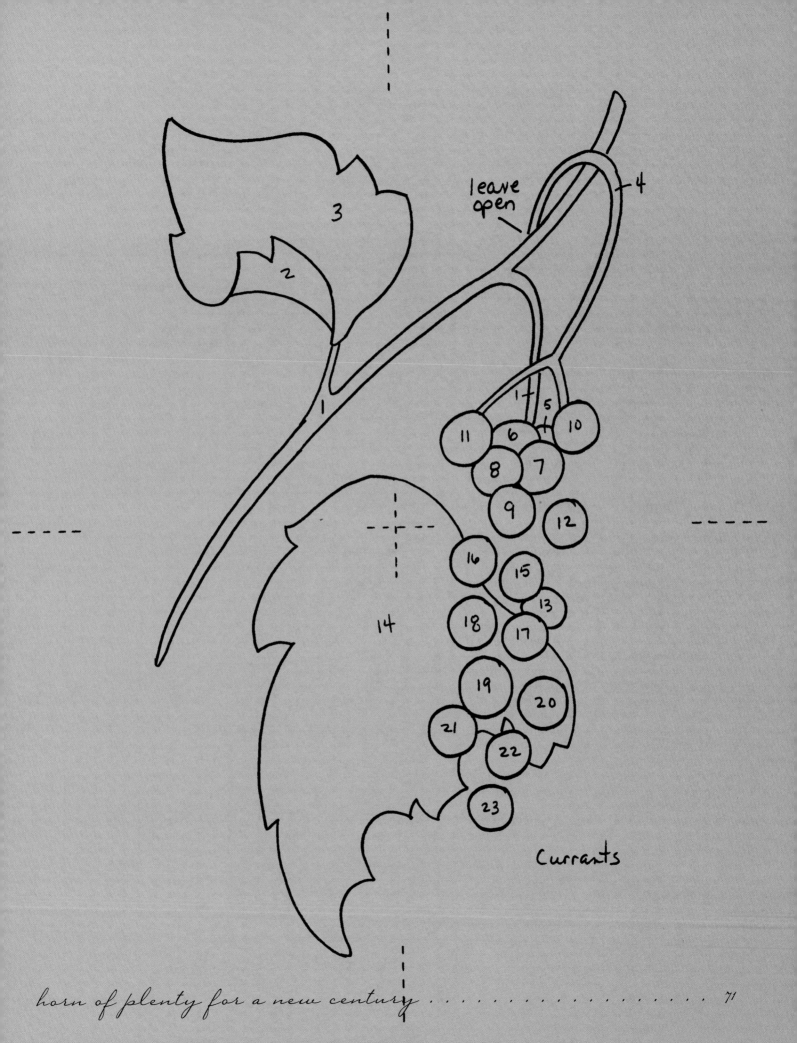

leave open

Currants

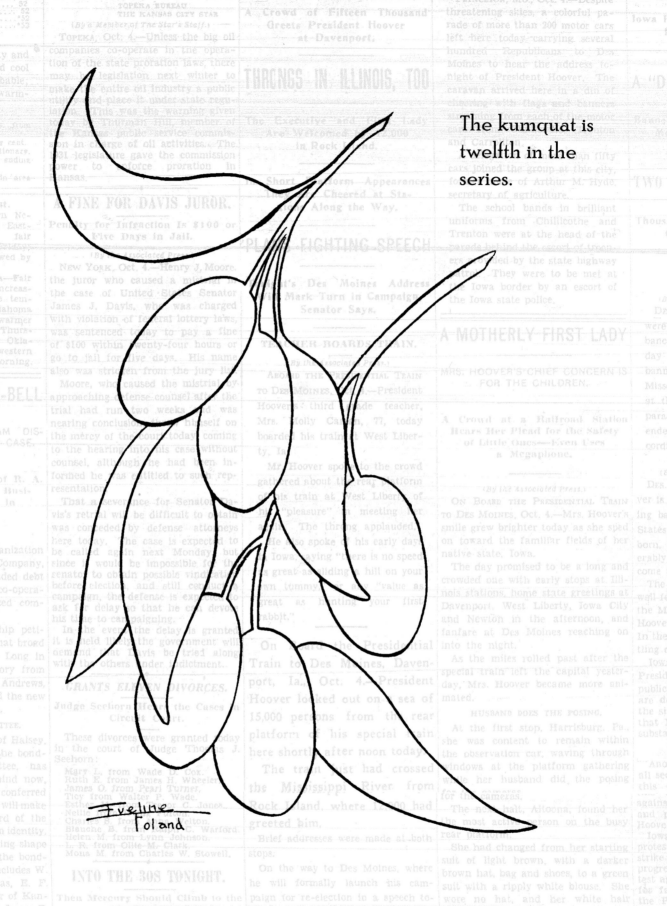

The kumquat is twelfth in the series.

Eveline Toland

THE KUMQUAT

*(The following directions appeared with the original pattern
in The Kansas City Star, January 25, 1932.)*

The pungent kumquat — little sister to the orange — will form a
bright spot in the color scheme. It is No. 12 in the series. They
are bright orange in color and could be done in two tones. The
leaves should be done in three shades of green. The stems are
dark green. Allow for seams.

Techniques I used include:
Cutaway Appliqué
Piecing the Appliqué

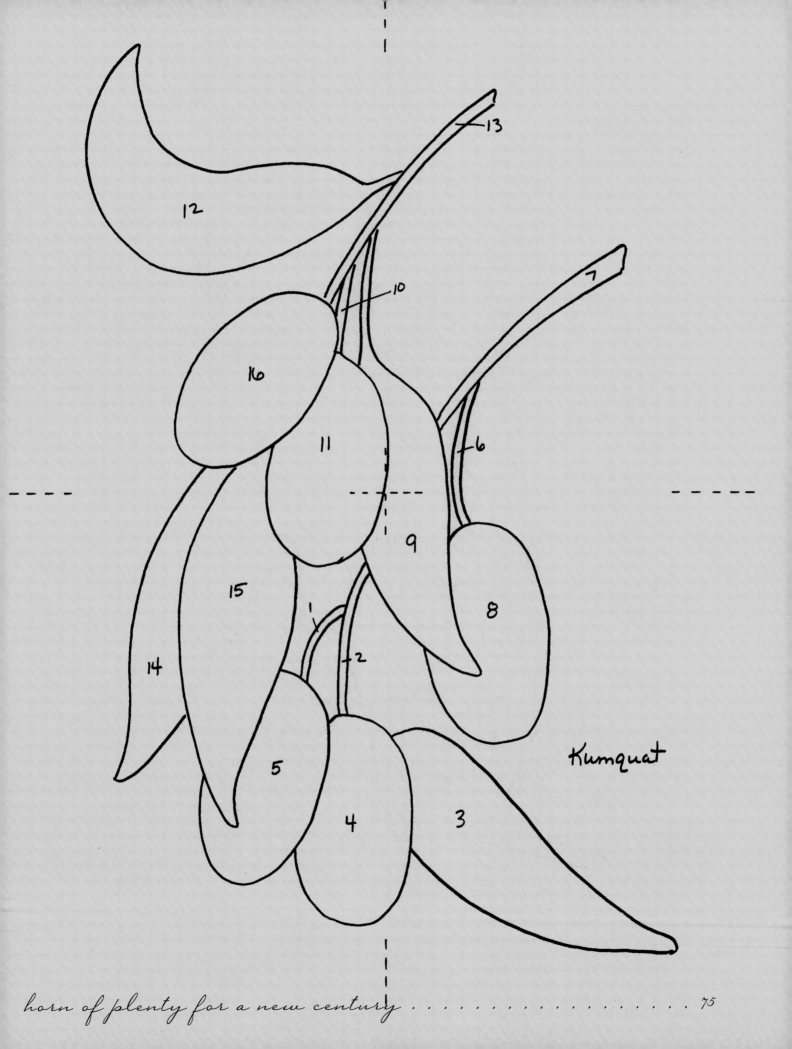

Kumquat

The cranberry is
a fruitful shrub.

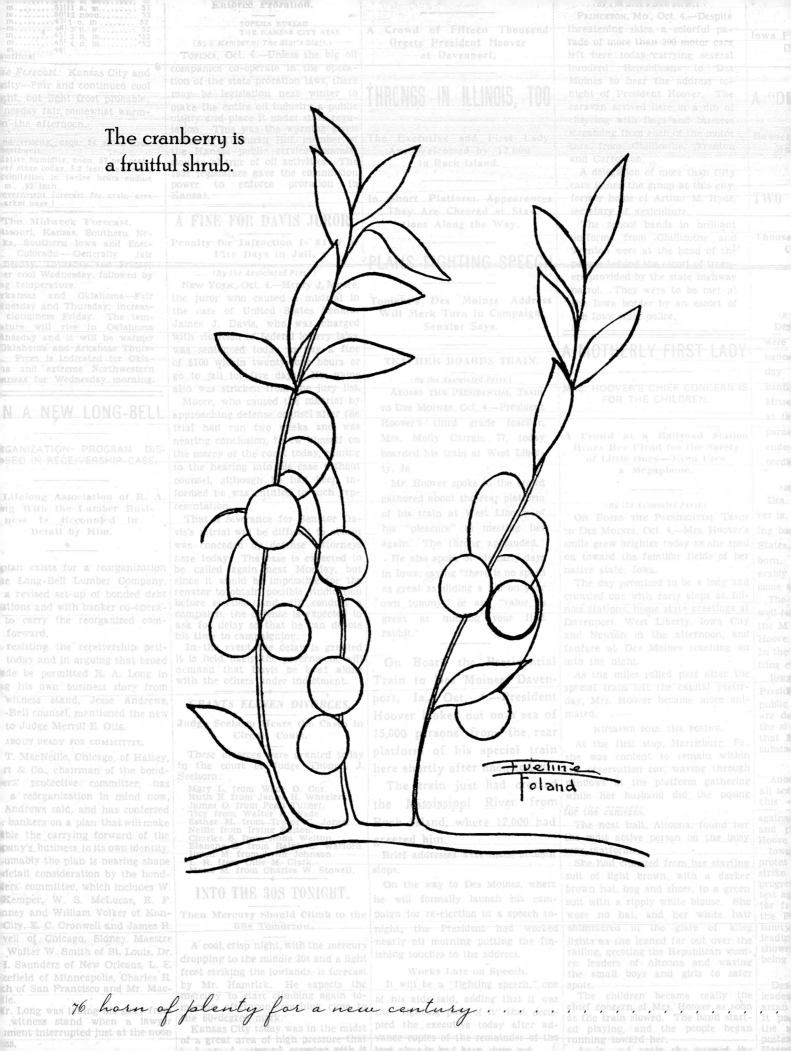

Eveline
Toland

THE CRANBERRY

(The following directions appeared with the original pattern in
The Kansas City Star, January 27, 1932.)

The jolly little cranberry is No. 13 in the Horn of Plenty quilt
series. What a tax on even the cleverest quilters to produce
a perfect piece of appliqué from this design.

The berries are light red — one or two almost pink — very
bright or cranberry red. The lighter berries are at the top. The
leaves may be a yellow pink at the top and shade from light
green to dark green at the bottom.

Techniques I used include:

Cutaway Appliqué

Template Form Circles

Piecing the Appliqué

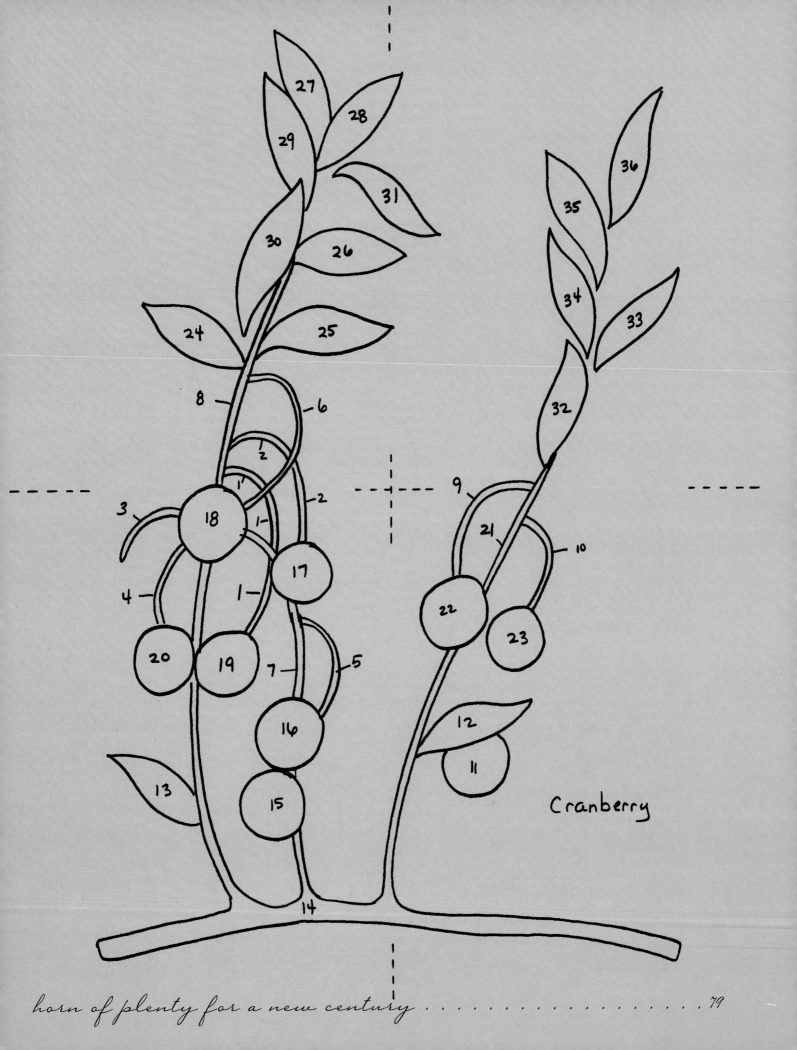

Cranberry

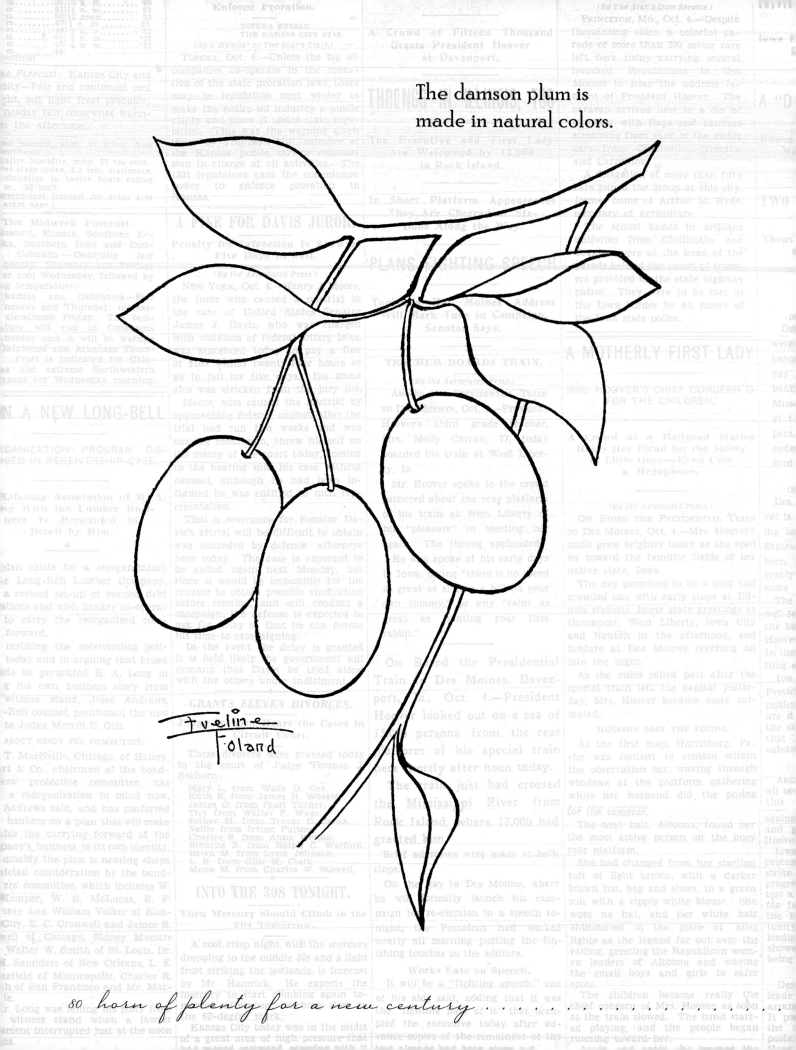

The damson plum is made in natural colors.

Eveline Toland

THE DAMSON PLUM

(The following directions appeared with the original pattern

in The Kansas City Star, February 1, 1932.)

The Damson plum is No. 14 in the Horn of Plenty quilt series

made in the dark bluish purple of the fruit. Allow for seams.

Techniques I used include:

Piecing the Appliqué

Cutaway Appliqué

The Twist #1

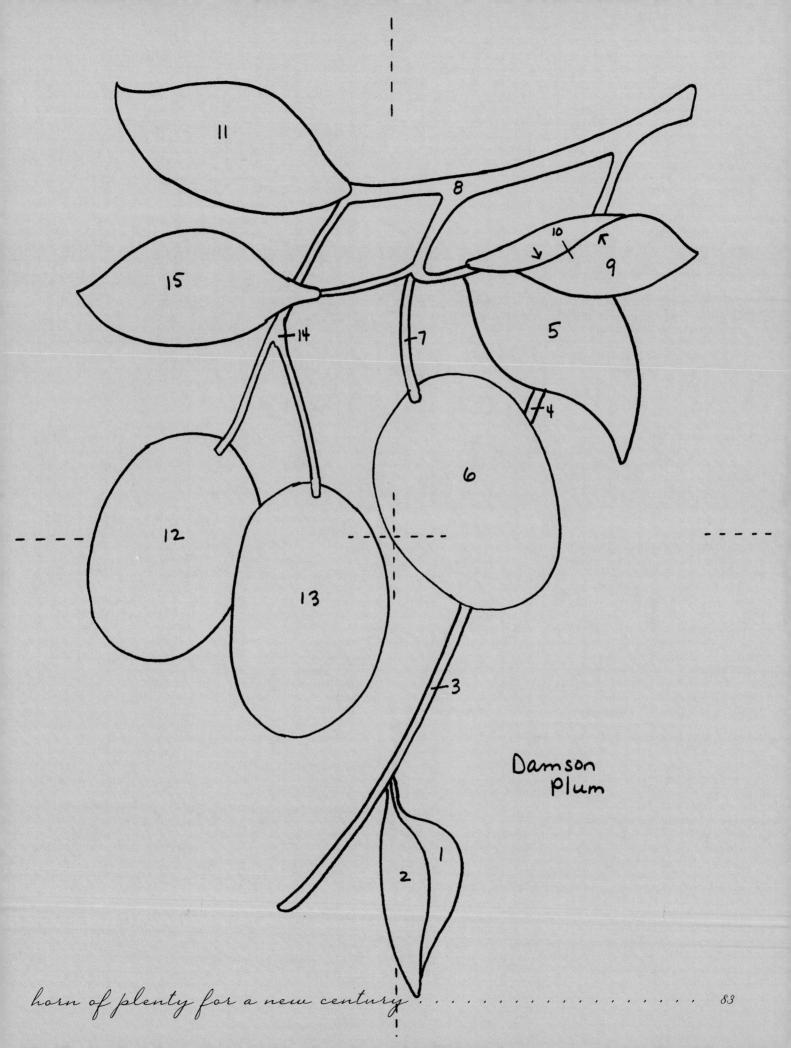

Damson
Plum

The loganberry may
be in its own red.

Eveline
Toland

THE LOGANBERRY

(The following directions appeared with the original pattern

in The Kansas City Star, February 5, 1932.)

The loganberry is No. 15 in the Horn of Plenty series, and may
be in its own wine red or lighter shades. Allow for seams.

◆

Techniques I used include:
Cutaway Appliqué
Combining Shapes
Reverse Appliqué

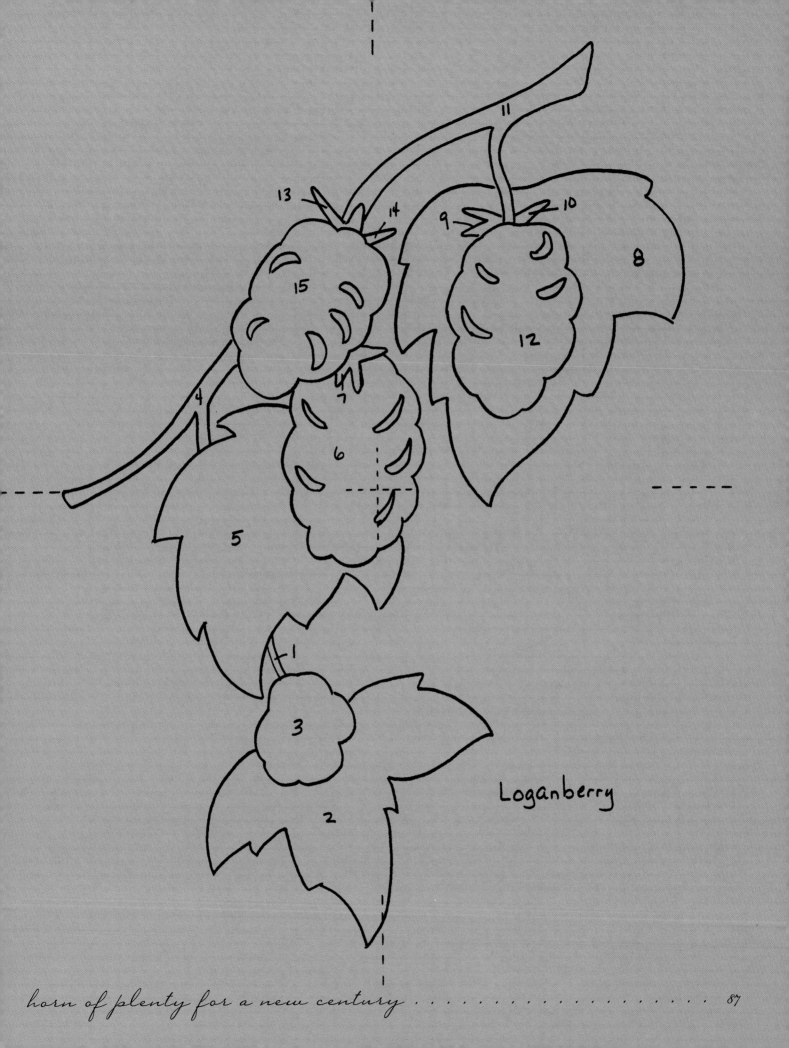

Loganberry

The yellow apple varies the array of fruits.

Eveline Toland

THE YELLOW APPLE

(The following directions appeared with the original pattern

in The Kansas City Star, February 8, 1932.)

This is the yellow apple which may be a pale blush color if so desired.

It is No. 16 in the Horn of Plenty series. Allow for seams.

Techniques I used include:

Cutaway Appliqué

Leave open

Piecing the Appliqué

Twist #1

The Twist #1

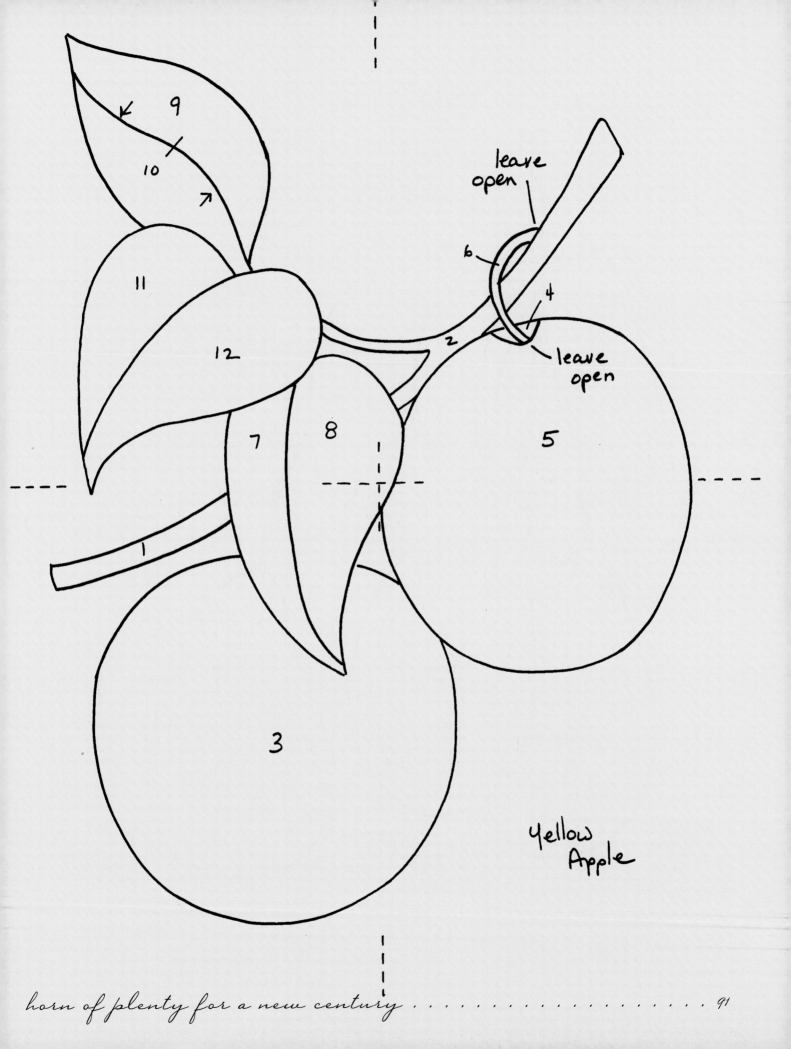

9

10

11

12

leave
open

6

4

leave
open

2

7

8

5

1

3

Yellow
Apple

The pear may be
the bright green
of the avocado.

Eveline
Foland

THE PEAR

(The following directions appeared with the original pattern

in *The Kansas City Star*, February 16, 1932.)

The avocado pear of bright green is one of the favorites of the winter market. This design may be in that color or it may be in the dusty brownish green shade of the orchard pear. Allow for seams.

Techniques I used include:
Combining Shapes
Cutaway Appliqué
Piecing the Appliqué
Reverse Appliqué
The Twist #1

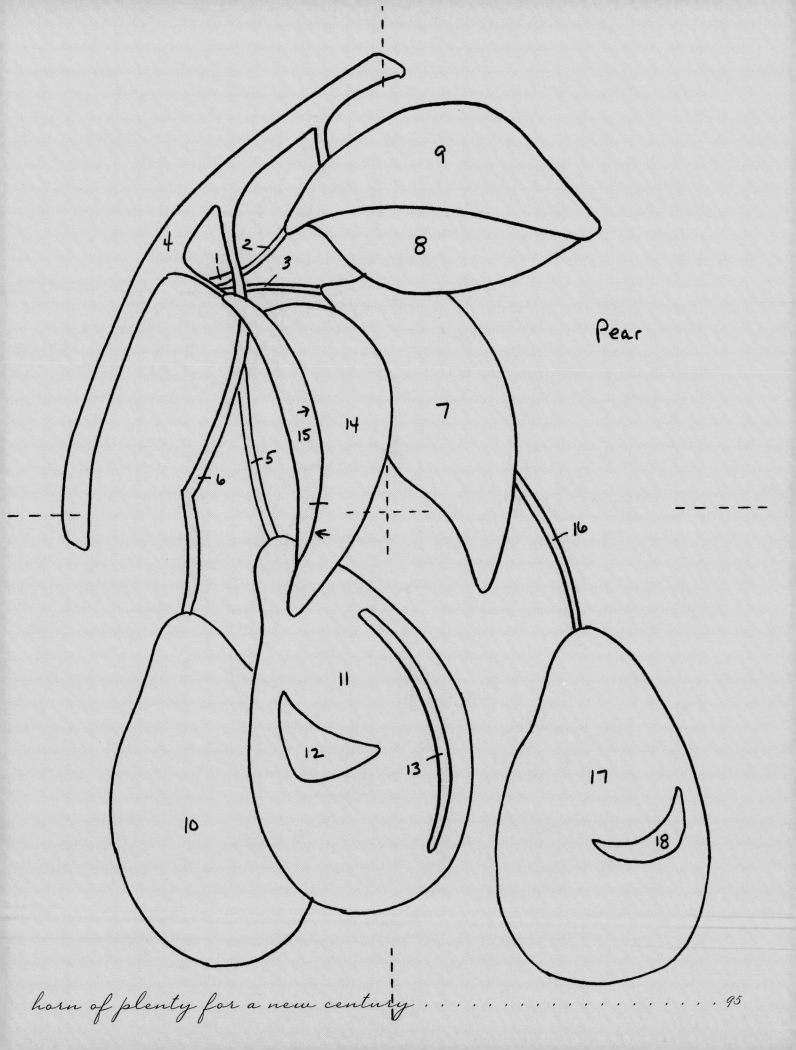

Pear

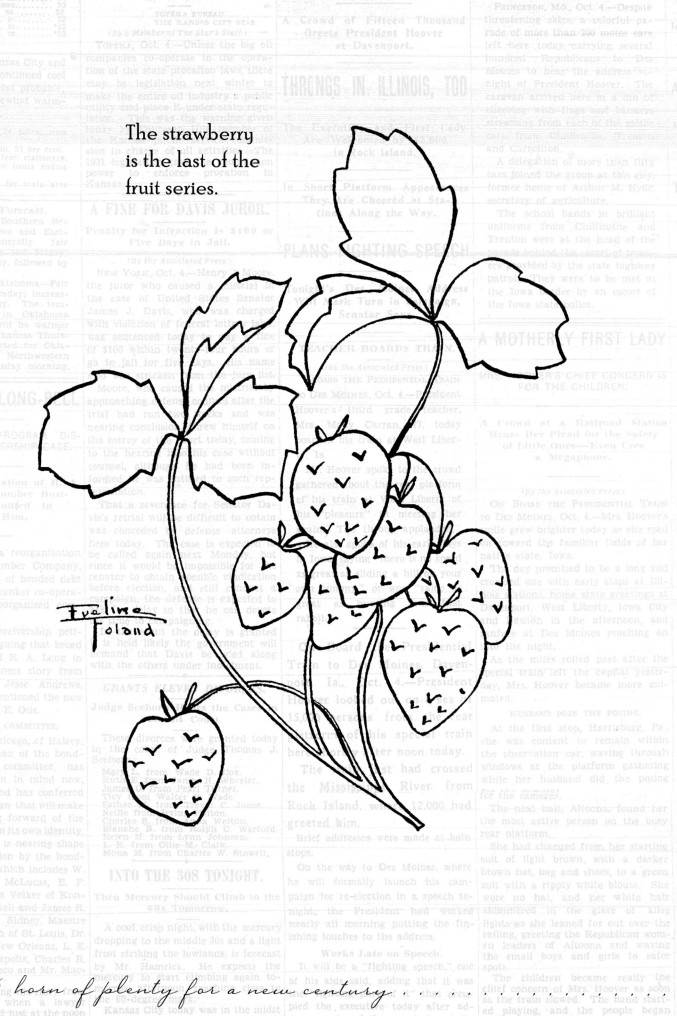

The strawberry is the last of the fruit series.

Eveline Toland

THE STRAWBERRY

(The following directions appeared with the original pattern

in The Kansas City Star, February 22, 1932.)

This is the last of the Horn of Plenty fruit blocks. The diagram, border and quilting design will follow as space permits. No need to tell this part of the world the colors for strawberries. Allow for seams.

◆

Techniques I used include:
Cutaway Appliqué
Piecing the Appliqué
The Twist #1

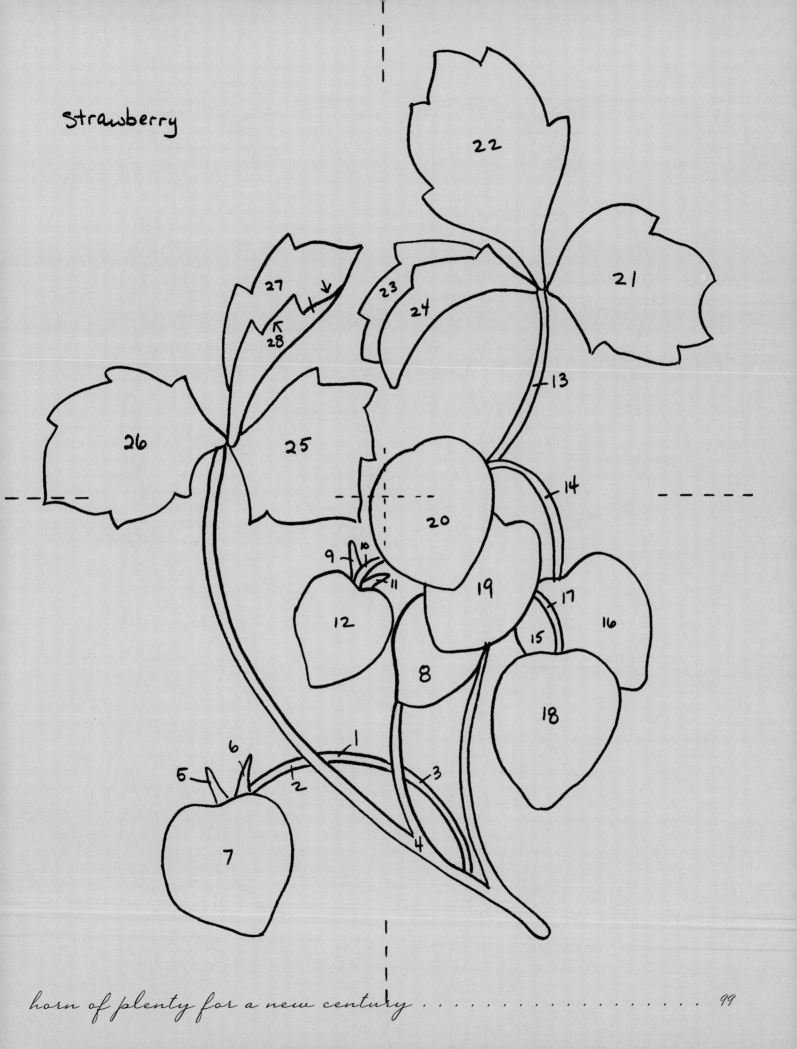

strawberry

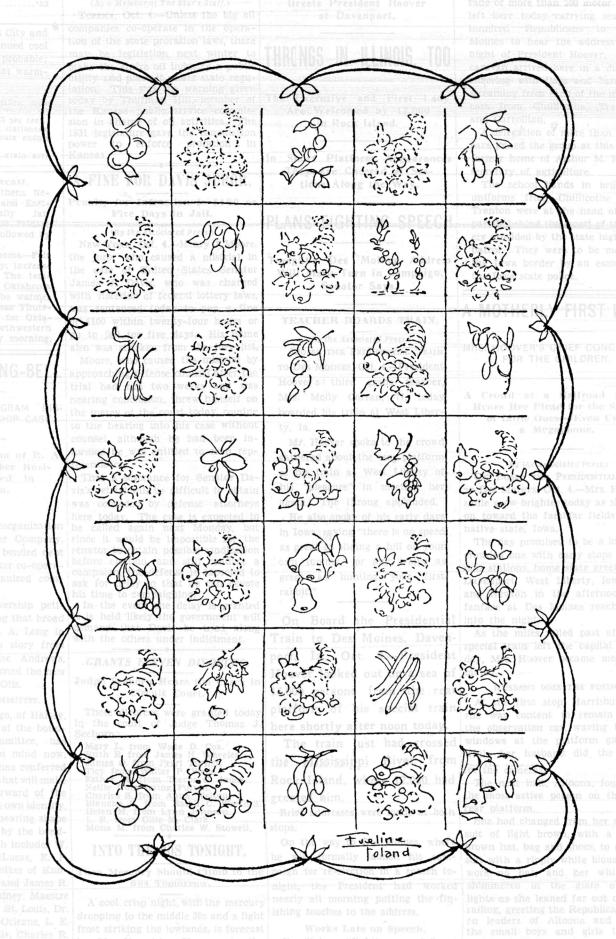

100 horn of plenty for a new century . . . .

Eveline
Toland

THE COMPLETE QUILT

(The following directions appeared with the original pattern in The Kansas City Star, February 25, 1932.)

This suggested arrangement of the fruit blocks of the Horn of Plenty quilt with alternate blocks (is) quilted in the Horn of Plenty quilting motif. The space between the blocks may be quilted in a diagonal pattern or a series of circles.

When the blocks have all been appliquéd, it is time to square them up and trim the excess. Begin by giving them a good pressing. I don't mean you will be ironing! No, ironing is best left for shirts. Set the iron down on the block and lift and then set it down again until the whole surface is pressed free of wrinkles.

Place the block, right side down, on your ironing board that has been covered with a clean, fluffy, terrycloth towel. The towel allows the appliqué to sink down into the softness and maintain its dimension. Press the back with your iron. I use steam while there are quilters who don't. Decide what works best for you. Just remember to press, do not iron.

A 12 1/2" square rotary cutting ruler is very handy for squaring your blocks. Use your placement overlay to find the horizontal center of the design. Place the 12 1/2" square ruler over the block, aligning the horizontal center with the 6 1/4" mark on the ruler. Trim the top and bottom with your rotary cutter.

Find the vertical center of the design and place the ruler so the 7 3/4" mark is over the vertical center, taking care to align the top and bottom edge of the ruler with the trimmed top and bottom of the block. (If you are left handed, place the 4 3/4" mark on the vertical center.) Trim the excess. Turn the block 180 degrees and place the trimmed edge under the 3" mark on the 12 1/2" square ruler, aligning the top and bottom of the block with the top and bottom edges of the ruler, and trim the excess. (If you are left handed, place the 9 1/2" mark on the trimmed edge.)

From the remainder of the background fabric you will need to cut (17) 9 1/2" x 12 1/2" rectangles. Arrange the appliquéd blocks with the alternate blocks and sew the rows together. Press the seam allowances in opposite directions so the odd numbered rows will all be pressed in one direction and the even numbered rows will all be pressed in the other direction.

When the blocks have all been sewn together, measure through the center both vertically and horizontally. If you sew with a consistent 1/4" seam allowance, your top should measure 63" x 60".

The border of
the quilt closes
the series.

Eveline Foland

THE BORDER

(The following directions appeared with the original pattern

in The Kansas City Star, February 26, 1932.)

This border design may be used on the Horn of Plenty quilt
or on any other. It has a simple leaf design for decoration.
As the quilt is elaborate, the border is simple. A quilt border
is a frame for a picture and should not compete in interest
with motifs of the quilt. This design closes the series which
consisted of eighteen fruit designs, one quilting design, one
diagram and one border.

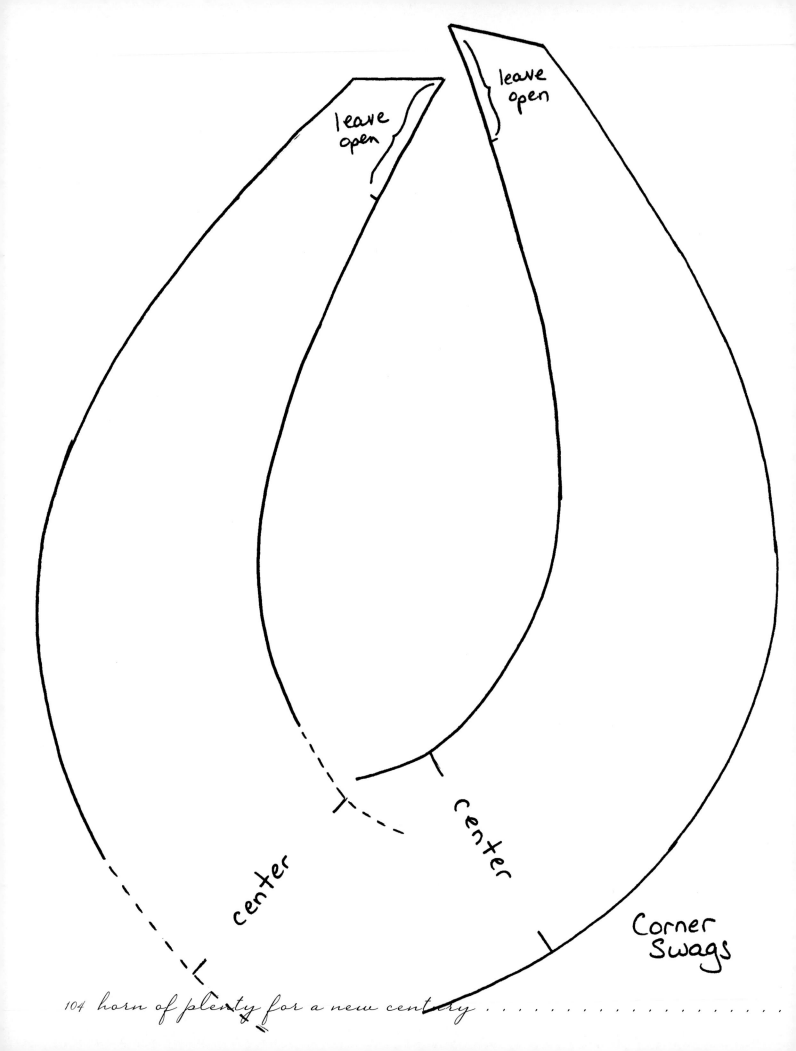

leave open

leave open

center

center

Corner
Swags

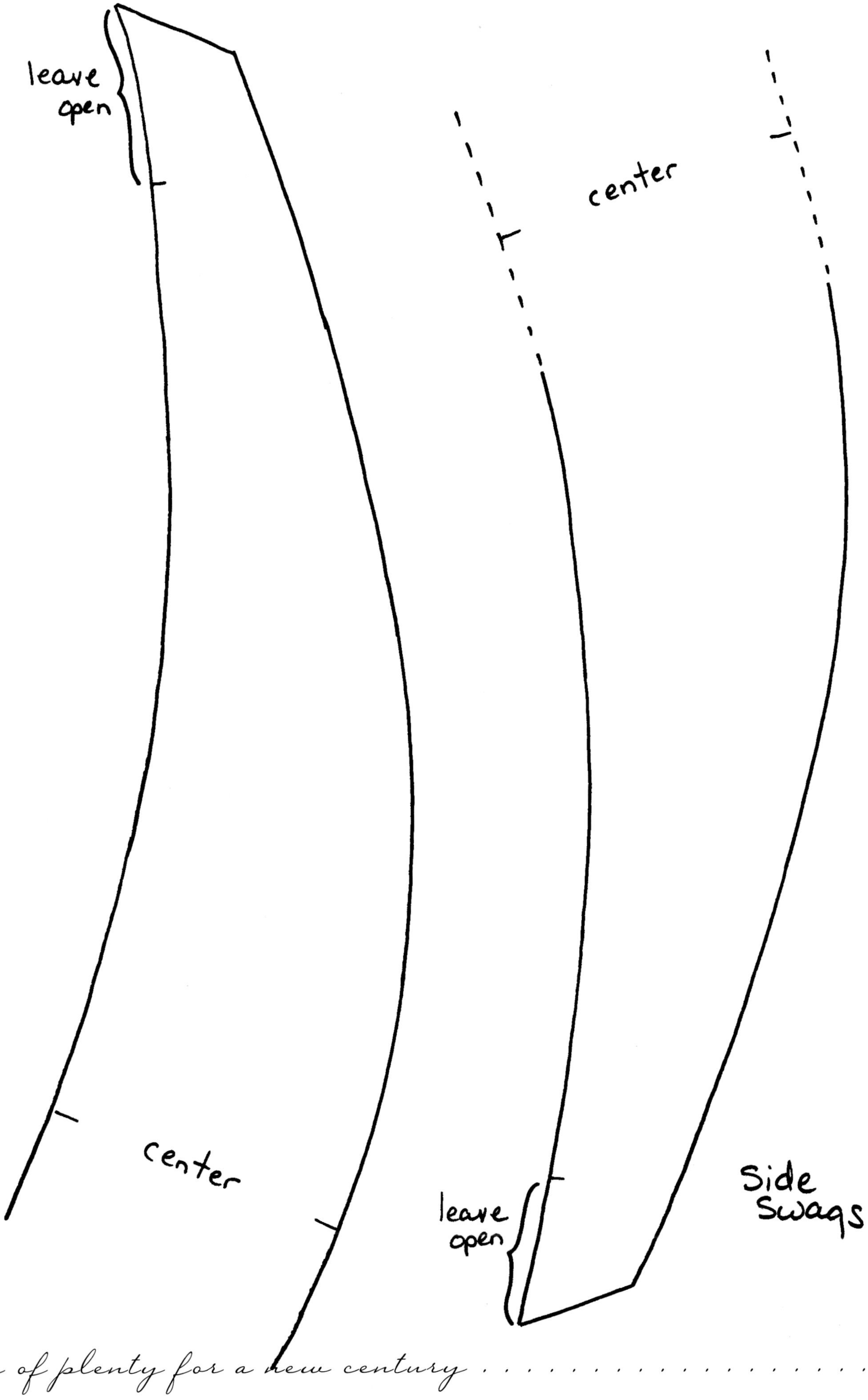

leave
open

center

center

leave
open

Side
Swags

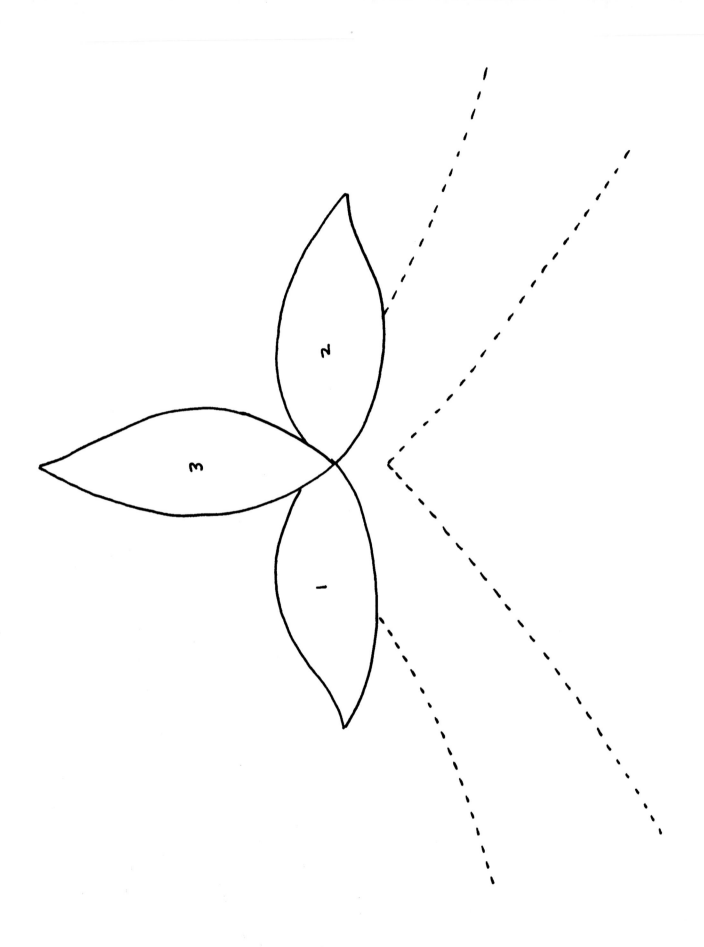

I find it much easier to add appliqué to the border strips before adding the borders to the quilt top. Cut border fabric into 10" strips the length of the fabric. Remove the selvages and fold the fabric so you have four layers, the full length of the fabric. The length of the strips should be 63" (or your longest measurement) plus twice the width of the borders (20") and then add a couple of inches for good measure. I recommend you cut them about 85" long if your quilt measures 63" through the center.

The swag templates can be placed on the fabric so they are stacked on the straight of grain. Even though the very center is on the straight of grain, the edges will be mostly on the bias. When you trace the swag shape you will notice a "leave open" note. In this case, it is not to place something under it. This time you want to leave the seam allowance unturned. This will eliminate bulk when you appliqué the leaves over that spot. (3-1)

3-1

Find the center of one of the border strips and mark it. You will be working from the center out to the ends. Two swags will meet in the center. If you have changed the size of your quilt, you will have to make adjustments to the length of the swags so they fit your border by taking a pleat in the center, removing length or splitting the center to add length. All instructions on these pages are going to assume that your quilt has the same dimensions as mine.

For a scalloped border, the swag appliqué touches the edge of the border strip and the bottom corners of the ends are 3 7/8" from the strip's edge. If you plan to have a straight edge on your quilt, you will want to place it in from the edge so there is background between the swag and the binding. Take a look at Tresa Jones' quilt on page ii and you'll see what I mean.

Turn under the seam allowance and appliqué the top edge of the swag for the scalloped edge. Baste the bottom edge without turning under the seam allowance. (3-2) The binding will be applied, covering the bottom, raw edge of the scallop. A straight edged quilt will require you to turn under the bottom edge as well.

Only appliqué the four side swags to each of the border strips at first. You will have to add the corner swags after sewing the borders to the quilt top. The corners of the border are mitered.

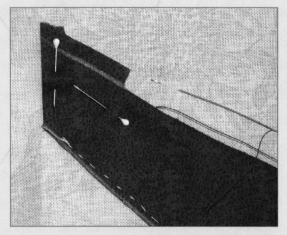

3-2

Begin by finding the center of one of the sides of your quilt top and mark it. I just place a pin. Then find the center of your border strip and mark it. Again, I use a pin. Measure through the center of your quilt top. Let's say it measured 63". Measure from the center marking of the border strip to the end 31 1/4" and mark with another pin. Repeat in the other direction. Match the three marks to your quilt top. Notice that the last two marks you made match 1/4" in from the corner. With a 1/4-inch seam allowance, sew from the 1/4-inch mark on one end to the 1/4-inch mark on the other. Press the seam allowance toward the border strip.

Sew each of the border strips on in this manner. Each time though, do not sew all the way to the end but stop 1/4" from the end. I suggest you backstitch at the spot you stop sewing to secure the strips while you are working on the mitered corners.

Once the border strips are added to the quilt top you are ready for the corner mitering. Begin by folding the quilt top on the diagonal at one corner, right sides together. Let us assume that you are folding the right side down to meet the bottom. The idea is to match the seams that hold the border strip to the quilt top. The border strips should lie one on top of the other, right sides together. I pin the seams so I know they stay matched as I move the quilt top under my sewing machine. (3-3)

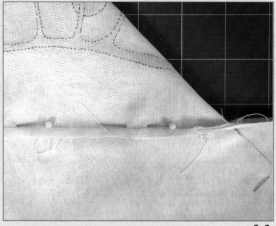

3-3

Place a large ruler, such as a 6" x 24" rotary cutting ruler, so the edge of the ruler lines up with the diagonal fold and extends over the border strips. You might also check to see that the edge of the ruler is on a 45-degree diagonal from the seams you have secured with pins, using the 45-degree mark on the ruler. (3-3a) Draw a line on the border strip that corresponds with the edge of the ruler. Move the ruler away, but before moving the quilt top, pin in several places across the drawn line. (3-3b)

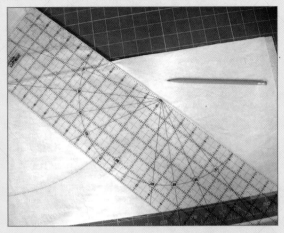

3-3a

Repeat these steps with each of the three remaining corners and you will be ready for quilting.

3-4

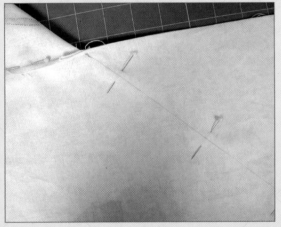

3-3b

Take the quilt top to your sewing machine and sew right on the line, from the raw edge in to the seam. You may want to backstitch a stitch or two at the spot the three seams come together in the corner.

At your ironing board, remove the pins and lay the corner of the quilt out flat and open the seam you just sewed. Press open and then remove the excess, leaving a 1/4" seam allowance.

The quilting design for the Horn of Plenty quilt.

Eveline Foland

QUILTING

(The following directions appeared with the original border

in The Kansas City Star, February 24, 1932.)

This design for quilting the alternate blocks of the Horn of Plenty quilts is so arranged that it will present a beautiful block for fine quilting. Cut each block 10 by 12 inches. If the white fabric used as a background is fine enough it may be placed over the paper and the pattern traced in the middle of the block. Otherwise, use carbon paper for tracing.

Quilt patterns often finish by saying, "Quilt as desired." I used to wonder just what that meant. Weren't there rules? Is there not a specific technique? Eventually I came to understand that while there are "rules" and specific techniques, there is no one way to quilt! I realized that the batting and the quilt top are going to be the determining factors regarding the amount and style of quilting.

Whether you hand quilt or machine quilt will determine which batting you use. While a polyester batting is easier to hand quilt, a cotton batting is more optimal for machine quilting as it does not let the top and bottom layers shift as easily even though basted. Your batting will also determine how much quilting your quilt will require. Be sure to check the package directions for the optimal distance between quilting lines. My favorite batting to use when hand quilting is a wool batting. Wool affords little resistance to the needle. I have often heard the sentence, "It quilts like butter." I have always imagined a very difficult task when the statement is taken literally unless the needle is hot enough to melt the butter! The Legler Barn quilters often commented that they were very glad I chose wool for my Horn of Plenty quilt!

You may wonder about what appears to be a yellow border on my quilt in some of the instructional photographs of the quilt before the binding is added. Putting a quilt on a large quilting frame, or even just in a smaller lap hoop, can cause increased tension on the edges of the quilt top. My friend Linda Mooney always puts an extra strip of fabric on all four sides to take up that added tension. So I tried it, too, and am glad I did. The edge of my quilt maintained its shape much better than it would have otherwise. Because the extra fabric is usually a scrap from some other project, it can look very strange.

"The Horn of Plenty" originally came with a quilting design for the alternate blocks. The Cornucopia really is a wonderful design and looks great quilted. When The Legler Barn Quilters and I were planning the quilting for my quilt, the original plan called for a 1-inch diagonal grid behind all of the appliqué designs and the Cornucopia designs. As we worked we discovered that the elements of the Cornucopia and the grid were so similar in size that the Cornucopia designs disappeared. So we switched to the two-inch grid in the center of the quilt. That helped to make those Cornucopia designs pop! Remember to let the quilt speak to you and listen!

We basted a line about 1/8" from the raw edge of the swag through all three layers of the quilt sandwich. This helped stabilize the three layers while the binding was applied since the quilting didn't actually reach all the way to the edge.

There are several ways to transfer a quilting design to your quilt top. Using a light box under the fabric with the pattern between and tracing is one way. Marking through a stencil cut into plastic is another. Tracing shapes cut from plastic is still another. But what do you do if the design you want to use is in a book, like this one?

Go to a garment-sewing center and ask for nylon net. You don't want the net that is as fine as bridal tulle but one that has a larger weave, such as a net you might have used for a really fluffy slip under your poodle skirt back in the 50's. It does not matter what color you choose. Notice the difference between the bridal tulle and the one I recommend in the photograph. (3-5)

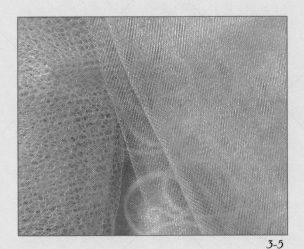

3-5

Begin by covering your quilting design with a clear plastic wrap from the kitchen drawer. I suggest you use a repositioning tape to secure the wrap. When you are ready to remove it, the paper pattern won't tear. You might even try the clear wrap that adheres when pressed against a surface.

The plastic wrap will protect the original design while you trace. Then, with a permanent marker, trace the design onto the nylon net. (3-6)

When you are ready to mark the quilting design on the quilt top, place the nylon net on the right side of the fabric, then trace the design with your fabric marker. The larger net lets your marking reach the fabric of the quilt top.

3-6

I cannot tell you what the perfect marker will be. If I could, I think I'd be able to retire to my very own quilting island! You will want to test your markers on the quilt fabric before marking your design. Each fabric releases the various markers (or not!) in their own fashion. Testing before you mark will save you from so much frustration. Don't think that the marker that worked so well on your last quilt project will work on this one! Maybe it will, and maybe it won't. Test your fabric and your markers each time you plan to mark a quilting design.

Scalloped Binding

A scalloped edge to a quilt gives it such a lovely look. While the scalloped edge is not the most difficult quilting technique, it does require some patience to achieve.

The first thing to consider is how much fabric you need for the binding. It is so straightforward to determine the fabric needs on a straight binding, but the scallop can be tricky. I have searched high and low for an easy mathematical formula to determine the fabric needs. Everyone I've talked to offers the very same solution that I came up with myself.

Begin by choosing a scallop. In the case of our quilt we have two different shaped scallops - the side scallops and the corners. They each may measure differently.

To measure a scallop, I might use a length of trimmed selvage I have saved from piecing lengths of fabric together for a backing. I can use a piece of string or a flexible measuring tape, too. Place the measuring device around the edge of a scallop and then measure the length of the string or tape. Multiply that measurement by the number of the scallops that size and you have the partial length of the outside edge of your quilt. (You'll notice in the photograph that my scallop measures 17 1/2" from end to end. It won't hurt for me to round that up to 18" per scallop.) (3-7) In the same way measure the four corners and add that to your first measurement and you'll have the full perimeter of the quilt.

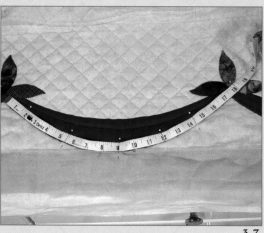

3-7

Because of the curves of the scallops, you will want to make your binding strips from bias-cut strips. The trick is to determine how large a piece of fabric you'll need to begin. At your local quilt shop you may find charts that give predetermined fabric requirements. There are some books that may have them but I have not found too many places that will tell you how those numbers were determined. I'd like to give you an idea of how to figure your own requirements.

The binding I recommend is a double folded binding for durability. Most of my binding strips begin as 2" or 2 1/4" strips. On occasion I use 2 1/2" strips, but only if the batting has a little higher loft or the fabric is a little thicker, such as flannel. I used a 2 1/4" strip for my Horn of Plenty quilt.

To determine the amount of bias binding fabric you need for your scalloped quilt, multiply the perimeter of your quilt by the width of the bias strip you'll use. Take a look at your calculator. Do you see the button with a square root symbol $\sqrt{}$ or perhaps the letters "sqrt"? Either one is the button that will find the square root of the number that appears in the display window. Hit that button after you multiply the perimeter by the strip width. Now, round that number up to the next highest even number and you will have the size of the square of fabric that you'll need to make the binding.

Let's see how this works. Let's say your side scallops measure 18" and there are four on each side of the quilt and the corner scallops measure 20" at each corner. That means your perimeter is 368 inches. Let's say you will want your bias strips to measure 2 1/4" wide. When you multiply the two numbers you get 828. The square root of 828 is 28.774. So we round that up to the next highest even number and we get 30 inches. We want a 30" square which means you need to purchase 7/8 yard of the binding fabric.

When you slice that 30" piece of fabric into bias strips, you will notice you have several strips from opposite corners that will be shorter than the majority of strips. I prefer to have the strips as long as possible and not use the short strips. Short strips mean many seams. I always plan to purchase an extra 3/4 to 1 yard of my binding fabric. I don't mind having leftovers but I do mind those seams. I buy extra so I can get most of the strips I need out of the full width of the fabric. If you measure one of the strips, divide that into the perimeter (remember that 828 inches we came up with in the example?) you'll find how many strips you need. I always add an extra strip for good measure so I'll have plenty for the final join.

I must fold the fabric in half on the bias so I am able to cut across the full width of the fabric on the bias. I don't have a ruler long enough to cross the full width of fabric, which is about 62". I don't even have a ruler that will cross the half, actually. You may be tempted to make the fold twice. To do that you must be very careful that both folds are perfectly parallel or you will end up with a W of a strip instead of a straight strip. I don't trust myself to make both folds line up that way, so I just make the one fold. Instead, I use two rulers, end to end, and cut very carefully and slowly, walking my anchoring hand up the ruler as the rotary cutter becomes parallel to my fingertips. (3-8)

3-8

There are directions in various places for making a "continuous bias" strip. This involves cutting a square (we are working with a rectangle) in half on the diagonal and sewing the two pieces back together again, altering the grain of the piece. Then you draw lines every 2 1/4", sew the ends together matching the lines but skewing them, creating a spiral, and then cut the line around the spiral. Doing so results in a continuous bias strip. For such a large piece of fabric, I would rather cut the strips with my rotary cutter and rotary cutting ruler. I really don't mind sewing the strips, end to end. (3-9) This is a matter of preference and you should do what is best for

you. Either method is correct.

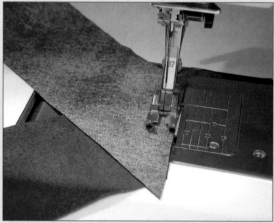

3-9

Once your binding strips are sewn together, press the seam allowances open, trim to 1/4 inch and press the strip in half, wrong side in, the full length of the binding. Be sure as you press the crease in you don't stretch the strips. Don't iron, press ~ up and down motions with the iron, not side to side.

Leaving a 12" or 15" tail, begin pinning the raw edges of the binding to the edge of the scallop on the downside of the scallop. (3-10) Don't begin at the highest point of the scallop but about halfway between the highest and lowest point. Please note, as I begin, I have not trimmed any of the excess away. I always trim after I have sewn on the binding, whether it is a straight binding or a scalloped edge. As you pin the binding to the curve of the scallop, be very careful that you do not stretch the binding by pulling it. The raw edge will stretch a little because you are making a straight edge curve. However, there is a fine line you must not cross. Think of the binding strip as three layers. The first layer, the raw edge, will stretch slightly in its space. The second layer, the body of the strip will not stretch at all. The third layer, the folded edge, will actually scrunch a little. This is a very good thing because when the folded edge gets pulled to the back, it needs to be able to stretch a little.

3-10

Pin only as far as the first pivot point, the deepest part of the V created between scallops and begin sewing. I recommend a 1/4- or 3/8-inch seam allowance, depending on how wide you made your bias strips. I use my even feed foot on my sewing machine (I always use the even feed foot for sewing on my binding) and sew very slowly. I do sew over my pins. I know that one is NOT supposed to. Machine makers just cringe at the thought! I once heard that if you have a new sharp needle, it is more likely to slide over the

side of a pin than hit it and break. I make sure I start with a new needle and I sew slowly. I've never broken a needle in this process. If you sew slowly enough, you can pull the pins just as you get to them so you won't sew over them. I recommend you leave the pin in until the needle is just about to sew over it, though. You don't want the fabric to shift, causing a pleat in the binding.

If your machine has a "needle down" setting, set it for down. This way as you stop sewing, the needle stays in the lowest position. When you lift the foot to reposition your quilt, you won't have to worry that you've moved away from the line of sewing. If you don't have this setting on your machine, advance the wheel by hand until the needle is in its lowest position before you reposition. Be careful you don't tug on the quilt, pulling the needle to bend it. You'll break it for sure.

Sew until you get to the deepest point of the V and stop with the needle in its lowest position.

If the pins are still in the binding you've sewn, take them out. Now start pinning the next scallop. The folded edge of the binding will want to stand up a bit at the V but don't worry about it. Just remember you don't want to pull the binding to stretch it. Carefully pin the binding to the next scallop until you reach the next V.

To begin sewing, I recommend you turn the quilt and make one stitch parallel to the straight of the grain of the border and then pivot again to stitch the curve of the scallop. This one little stitch will relieve some of the stress that will be put on the pivot point. Before you begin stitching the next scallop, you will want to move the seam allowance of the sewn binding out of the way. To do this, use a stiletto, or even the tip of a seam ripper, to grip the seam allowance and fold it back on itself. Since it is basically under your feed foot, you won't be able to reach it with your finger. (3-11) Continue sewing the binding to your scallops all the way around your quilt, ending about halfway between the last V and the highest point of the scallop. You will again want a 12" to 15" tail.

3-11

I join the two ends in the same manner as I do when sewing a straight binding. Place the raw edges along the edge of the scallops until the two tails meet in the middle. Fold the tails back on themselves until the

fold meets. Now open the space between the two folds about 1/8 inch. (3-12) With small scissors, clip through the folds, no more than 1/4 inch. (3-13)

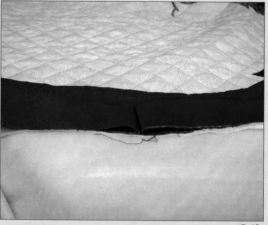

3-12

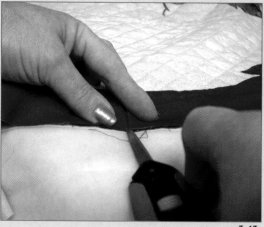

3-13

With the body of the quilt spread out on the table in front of you, right side up, and the binding tails right in front of you, open the left tail so the wrong side is up. Place your left hand just behind the tail, palm up. Flip the left tail onto your left hand so the right side is up. In essence, you have rotated the strip of fabric away from yourself.

Now open the right tail so the wrong side is up. Lay the right tail on top of the left tail. The right sides will be together.

Match the notches in the tails that you created by snipping through the folds. What's happening is that the bottom notch of the right tail is matched to the top notch of the left tail (1). The bottom notch of the left tail aligns with the bottom edge of the right tail (2). The top notch of the right tail aligns with the top edge of the left tail (3). Take a look at the photograph and you'll see what I mean. (3-14)

3-14

I always pin so the pins are aligned with the tails. When I sew across the tails, I can easily remove the pins. Sew from the V the crossing tails create, through the crossed tails, to the V on the other side. (3-15)

Press the seam open and trim the seam allowances to 1/4 inch. Fold the binding again and re-press. At this point you will be ready to finish attaching the binding to

the quilt. Align the raw edges of the binding with the edge of the scallop and finish stitching. You will have a smooth join without bulk.

3-15

When the binding has been sewn to the quilt top, trim the excess away from the edge of the scallops. I always trim about 1/16 to 1/8 inch from the raw edge. That little bit of extra batting will help fill the binding in case my stitching meandered slightly from 1/4-inch seam allowance. (3-16)

3-16

Fold the folded edge of the binding to the back of your quilt and hand stitch with an invisible stitch to secure, hiding the machine stitching. Match your thread to the binding to camouflage the stitching.

When you get to the V at the deepest part of the scallops you will want to miter the binding. Clip into the V, clipping through all the layers of the seam allowance. You do not need to clip all the way to the stitching, just about halfway. This clip gives you some working room with the fold that will be created in the binding. As you get to the deepest part of the V, take a tuck in the binding so you have a nice crisp point in the V. I make the tuck on the back in the opposite direction of the tuck on the front. Stitch the fold the tuck creates just as you do on the corners of the straight, mitered binding corners, front and back. (3-17) Your binding will be very neat and the edge of your quilt will look very crisp.

3-17

The quilt in the basket made by Kelly Herl, Springhill, KS , 2004

CHAPTER FOUR
Projects

According to Eveline Foland, you can "use designs for cushions, for decorative motifs for painted furniture, for drawing lessons for the children or any other use an artistic fruit design may fulfill." My friend Connie Coffman told me decorating with fruit is appropriate in any room you are comfortable eating fruit. I hope you find some fun decorating ideas within these pages!

The projects on the following pages are meant to give you some ideas for using different techniques with these appliqué patterns.

Instead of chenille pillows, you might combine the pillow tops into a throw that is totally chenilled for a cozy winter wrap. Choose several of the fruits or duplicate the apples and oranges on several blocks.

Try your hand at creating your own unique design for the "Tropical Lemons" pillow. Use the techniques described to appliqué your own fruit "snowflake".

Most importantly, have some fun!

"To Market" Tote
22" x 23" x 5"
Made by Kim Morrow, Overland Park, KS, 2004.

"TO MARKET" Tote
22" x 23" x 5"

Fabrics needed: *(I recommend you have some FUN and choose fabrics that contrast yet coordinate with each other. Your tote may be bright and fun or elegant or subtle.)*
- 1/3 yard for pocket (lining included) (or you may choose 2 fat quarters so the inside is different from the outside)
- Assorted scraps for appliqué motif
- 1/3 yard for handles
- 5/8 yard for tote exterior
- 5/8 yard for tote lining
- 1/8 yard for interior binding
- (2) 1 1/2" x 66" pieces of batting-low loft (may splice but no farther than 18" from either end so handle doesn't "break")
- (1) 9 1/2" x 14 1/2" piece of batting (optional)
- (2) 20" x 19" pieces of batting (low loft)

Appliqué pocket

From the pocket fabric cut (2) 9 1/2" x 15" rectangles. On the right side of one of the rectangles appliqué the fruit pattern of your choice using the method you like best. I recommend raising the horizontal center about 2 or 2 1/2 inches. The bottom 2 or 2 1/2 inches of the block are actually on the bottom surface of the tote. (Kim's sample is needleturn appliquéd and embroidered and includes decorative buttons to represent cherries.)

With right sides together, sew the appliqué and lining along the top edge only with a 1/4" seam allowance. Press the seam allowance toward the lining and top stitch next to the seam through the lining and the seam allowance. Press the two rectangles, wrong sides together, finishing the top edge.

If you wish, you can place a 9 1/2" x 14 1/2" piece of batting between the front and back panels of the pocket. Quilt around the appliqué and a simple grid across the background behind the appliqué.

Handles

From the handle fabric, cut (3) 3 3/4" strips from selvage to selvage. Remove the selvages and then cut one of the lengths into two equal parts. Sew a short length to each of the longer lengths at the short ends and press the seam allowances open.

Along one of the long edges of each of the handle strips, fold the edge 1/4" and press as for a hem. Lay the 1 1/2" wide pieces of batting on the center of the wrong side of the handle strips. Fold the raw, unhemmed, edge across the batting and bring the hemmed edge over the top of it. You will need to pin to stabilize while you are topstitching/quilting.

With your walking foot attachment, machine stitch through all layers right along the hemmed edge and then stitch 2 or 3 more rows of stitching down the full length of the handles. Zigzag stitch across the raw ends to secure and "flatten."

Tote

From the tote exterior fabric cut (2) 23" x 24" rectangles. From the tote lining fabric cut (2) 18" x 23" rectangles. Sew a lining rectangle to a tote rectangle along the 23" side, right sides together, with a 1/4" seam allowance. Press the seam allowance toward the lining and topstitch through the lining and seam allowances, next to the seam, to finish. Note the top of the lining of the tote, once the tote is constructed, will match the outside of the tote while deeper inside the tote will be a contrasting fabric. Repeat with the second pair of rectangles.

Place a piece of the 20" x 19" batting on the wrong side of the tote portion of the new units, centering the batting 1/2" away from the three raw edges. If you fold the tote/lining fabric in half, wrong sides together, and finger press you will easily be able to find the proper placement of the batting.

Fold the lining portion down over the batting, aligning the raw edges. The batting should fill the fold. Pin baste and quilt by machine through all three layers. I recommend a 2" diagonal grid for stability. You may hand quilt if you prefer, but remember the appliqué pocket covers most of one side so the quilting won't really show that much.

Center the pocket on the tote side of one of the quilted pieces, aligning the raw edges along the bottom. Topstitch 1/4" from the raw edge along the 2 sides of the pocket.

Place one of the handle straps over the right raw edge of the pocket, aligning the end with the bottom raw edge, and covering the stitching holding the pocket secure. Place the strap so the center seam is against the tote. Pin in place. Place the other end of the strap on the left raw edge of the pocket, aligning the end with the bottom raw edge, and covering the stitching holding the pocket secure. Again, the center seam is against the tote. The strap should allow between a 3 1/2" to 4" space to the side edges of the tote. Top stitch the straps along both edges of the strap to the tote. The topstitching will secure the straps to the tote as well as covering the raw edge of the appliqué pocket.

Repeat with the other strap and the back of the tote. The straps will be spaced in the same manner as are the straps framing the pocket so be sure to measure the space between the raw edge and the outer edge of the strap on the tote front. Top stitch the straps to the tote back to secure.

Place the two halves of the tote, right sides together, and sew around the three raw edges with a 1/4" seam allowance. You will have no batting in the seam allowances to add any bulk.

To finish the seams, cut (2) 2" x 40" strips from your binding fabric and sew them end-to-end, pressing the seam allowance open. Measure the side seams and bottom seam of your tote and cut the binding strip length to match, plus 2 inches. Press the strip, wrong sides together, in half along the full length.

Trim the seams on your tote so they are 1/4" wide. Attach the binding as you would on a quilt, beginning your stitching, however, about 1/2" from the end and leaving an inch extending past both ends. You will need to finish the ends by hand, folding the ends in and stitching the folds together, enclosing the raw edges.

To finish the bottom, pinch the side and bottom seams together at the lower right corner and draw a line, perpendicular to the seam, 3 inches from the tip. This will form a triangle. Stitch across the base of the triangle on the drawn line through the seam. Make sure the side seam allowance and the bottom seam allowance fold in opposite directions, eliminating bulk. Repeat on the lower left corner.

Fold the triangle "flaps" that were created toward the center. This will square off the bottoms of the tote. Whipstitch the flaps in place to secure, making sure that the point of the triangle lies on the seam.

Turn your tote right sides out and admire your work! You're finished!

To close your tote you may wish to add a loop and button at the top center or sew a "button" of hook and loop tape to the inside of the top edge in the center.

"Mixed Fruit Salad" Table Topper
46" x 46"
Made by Connie S. Coffman, Lenexa, KS 2004

"MIXED FRUIT SALAD" Table Topper
46" x 46"

Fabric needed:
- 1 yard light background (appliqué and baskets)
- 5/8 yard medium background (center background, basket handles, basket bases and binding)
- 3/8 yard focus print (baskets, large star, center pinwheel)
- Assorted scraps for appliqué
- 1 1/2 yards backing
- 50" x 50" low loft batting

Cutting instructions: (All cuts are taken across the grain, from selvage to selvage.)

Light Background –
- Cut (1) 12 1/2" wide strip and (1) 12 5/8" strip.
- From the first strip cut (3) 12 1/2" squares.
- From the second strip cut (1) 12 5/8" square and (1) 12 1/2" square. The (4) 12 1/2" squares are the appliqué background.
- Cut the 12 5/8" square in half diagonally in both directions so you have (4) quarter square triangles. These quarter-square triangles are the top half of the basket squares where you will appliqué the basket handles.
- Cut (2) 3 1/2" squares. Cut each square in half diagonally once so you have a total of (4) half-square triangles. These half-square triangles are the bottom corners of the basket backgrounds.

- Cut (8) 1 7/8" x 6 1/8" rectangles. Pair (2) rectangles, wrong side together, and trim one end of the pair with a 45-degree cut. Take care you do not shorten the rectangle. One edge will still be 6 1/8" long. You will have mirror images of the shape. Repeat with the remaining (3) pairs. These shapes are the side background pieces of the baskets.

Medium Background –
- Cut (1) 12 5/8" square. Cut this square in half diagonally in both directions so you have (4) quarter-square triangles. These quarter-square triangles are in the center of the large star.
- Cut (2) 6 1/2" squares. Cut each square in half diagonally once so you have (4) half-square triangles. These half-square triangles are background to the center pinwheel.
- Cut (1) 6 7/8" square. Cut this square in half diagonally in both directions so you have (4) quarter-square triangles. These quarter-square triangles are also background to the center pinwheel.
- Cut (4) 2 1/8" squares. Cut each square in half diagonally once so you have a total of (8) half-square triangles. These half-square triangles are the base of the baskets.
- Trace the basket handle template (shown on page 133) onto freezer paper (4) times on the non-shiny side. Do not add seam

allowance. Place the freezer paper templates onto the right side of the remaining fabric, shiny side down, leaving at least 1/2" between templates. Press with a hot, dry iron to temporarily adhere the templates to the fabric. Trace the template with the appropriate marker. Trim the excess fabric, leaving a 3/16" seam allowance along the sides of the handle and 1/4" seam allowance at the ends of the handles.

Focus Print –
• Cut (2) 12 5/8" squares. Cut the squares in half diagonally in both directions so you have (8) quarter-square triangles. These quarter-square triangles are the large star points.
• Cut (2) 6 1/8" squares. Cut the squares in half diagonally so you have (4) half-square triangles. These half-square triangles are the baskets.
• Cut (1) 6 7/8" square. Cut the square in half diagonally in both directions so you have (4) quarter-square triangles. These quarter- square triangles are the points of the center pinwheel.

Constructing the Blocks
This little quilt consists of (9) blocks and (4) half-blocks. Four of the blocks are the appliqué, four are Hourglass blocks, which make the large star points, and one is a Pinwheel. The half-blocks are the Baskets. (All seams are sewn with a 1/4-inch seam allowance.)

Appliqué blocks:
Choose the appliqué method and fruit pattern(s) of your choice and prepare your templates for appliqué.

Appliqué the designs onto the center of the (4) 12 1/2" squares. Set these blocks aside, without trimming until the other blocks are constructed.

Hourglass blocks:
For each of the four blocks you will need (2) quarter-square triangles from the focus fabric, (1) from the light background and (1) from the medium background.

Sew a light triangle to a focus triangle,

right sides together, along one of the bias edges. Sew a medium triangle to the other focus triangle, right sides together, along the same bias edge. In other words, if you orient the light to the right side of the triangle, the medium should be oriented to the right side of the other triangle. Press the seam allowances toward the focus fabric. As you press, avoid touching the other bias edge with the iron.

Matching the center seams, right sides together, sew the two triangle units together. Because you pressed the seam allowances to the focus fabric, the opposing seam allowances will allow you to make a snug match

.

Before pressing the seam allowance, turn the block over and notice the pressed seam allowances are in opposite directions. You are going to press the new seam in opposite directions, splitting the seam in the center at the intersection. To do this, loosen the first 2 or 3 stitches in the very center of the seam just sewn. Most of the time you can do this by holding the two halves of the seam just on either side of the intersection and giving it a twist. If that little twist will not break the stitch, then use your scissors and clip the first stitch or two.

You will be able to press the 2 halves of the seam allowance in opposite directions so the center will lie flat. All the seam allowances should be pressed in the same direction, rotating around the center point.

Appliqué the basket handles you prepared earlier to the light background quarter of each of the Hourglass blocks. Center the handles on the triangle and align the bottom edges of the handles with the edge of the block.

Pinwheel block:

For this block you will need the (4) smaller quarter-square triangles from the focus fabric, the (4) quarter-square triangles from the medium background and the (4) half-square triangles from the medium background fabrics.

Sew each of the medium quarter-square triangles to each of the focus quarter-square triangles in the same way you did for the Hourglass blocks. Press the seams toward the medium background, avoiding touching the iron to the bias edges. Each of the new triangle units should look exactly alike.

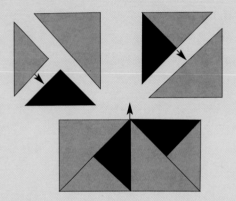

Sew each of the new triangle units to the medium half-square triangles and press the seam allowances toward the medium background. Trim the little extending seam allowance triangles so you have (4) units.

Sew two of the squares together. The base of the focus triangle of one square will align with the side of the larger medium triangle of the other square. Press the seam allowance toward the medium background.

Repeat with the second pair of squares.

With right sides together, match the center seams of the new units. Because you pressed the seam allowances to the background fabric, the opposing seam allowances will allow you to make a snug match.

Before pressing the seam allowance, turn the block over and notice the pressed seam allowances are all pressed in the same direction. You are going to press the new seam allowances in opposite directions, splitting the seam in the center at the intersection, so they too will rotate around the center. To do this, loosen the first 2 or 3 stitches in the very center of the seam just sewn. If that little twist will not break the stitch, then use your scissors and clip the first stitch or two.

You will be able to press the 2 halves of the seam allowance in opposite directions so the center will lie flat. All the seam allowances should be pressed in the same direction, rotating around the center point.

Baskets:

Sew a small half-square medium background triangle to the square end of each of the 6 1/8" rectangles as shown below. These are the background of the basket and the base of the basket.

Sew the new units to the non-bias edges of the focus triangle. Press the seams toward the focus triangle. Sew the background triangle to the base of the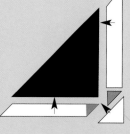

basket to complete the basket.

Putting it all together
Measure the Hourglass blocks and the Pinwheel block. If your seams were a consistent 1/4-inch, your blocks should measure 11 3/8" square. Trim your appliqué blocks so they are the same size as your pieced blocks.

Sew the basket units to the Hourglass blocks, right sides together, aligning the basket to the edge with the appliquéd handle. As you sew, place the Hourglass block on top of the basket as the pair moves over the feed dogs of your sewing machine to avoid stretching the bias edge.

Take a look at the finished sample on page 128, made by Connie Coffman. Notice the baskets are on the outside edges of the four sides. The quilt top consists of (3) rows of (3) blocks.

Sewing with a consistent 1/4-inch seam allowance will ensure all of the points are sharp. Sew the blocks to form (3) rows and then sew the rows together to finish the quilt top. When pressing your seam allowances, you will notice whatever way you press, you will be pressing intersecting seams, when trying to press in opposite directions. Since your appliqué blocks are a light background, you don't want the seams to shadow through. I suggest you press toward the focus fabric. This will allow you to press away from the pinwheel in the center row so you don't affect the points.

When pressing the seams that combine rows, you may find it easier to press away from the center. Again, this will ensure you don't lose your points on the Pinwheel.

Make a sandwich with the quilt top, batting and backing and baste, using your favorite method. I recommend you use a batting with a very low loft if you plan to use your quilt to top a table.

Quilt as you'd like. I suggest you quilt around each of the appliqué shapes to define them. A crosshatch design behind the appliqué would also enhance the appliqué but you should let your own aesthetic sense guide you.

To bind your quilt, refer to the scalloped binding directions beginning on page 114. While your edges are, indeed, straight and not curved, the method is the same. You have those inside corners which are treated the same way for both looks.

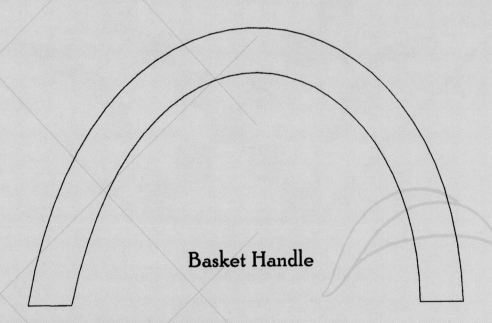

Basket Handle

"Lemonade Chain" Table Topper
30" x 30" hexagon
Made by Barbara Fife, Overland Park, KS, 2004.

"LEMONADE CHAIN" Table Topper
30" x 30" hexagon

Fabric needed:
- 1 fat quarter dark print
- 1/4 yard of the same dark print for binding
- 7/8 yard of light background
- Assorted scraps for appliqué
- 1 yard backing
- 34" x 34" batting

Cutting Instructions:
Dark Print -
- Cut (5) 2 1/2" x 22" strips.

Light background -
- Cut (2) 2 1/2" x 44" strips. Cut the strips in half so there are (4) 2 1/2" x 22" rectangles. You will need three of these pieces.
- Cut (1) 6 1/2" x 22" strip. Cut the strip in half so there are (2) 6 1/2" x 22" rectangles.

Light background -
- Cut (1) 14 1/4" square.
- Cut the square in half diagonally in both directions so you have (4) quarter-square triangles.
- Cut (1) 11 1/2" square.

Constructing the Blocks:
Framed Nine-Patch Blocks

Strip Set A -
Sew a print 2 1/2" x 22" strip to both edges of a light background 2 1/2" x 22" strip. Cut the strip set into (8) 2 1/2" x 6 1/2" rectangles.

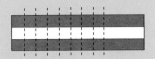

Strip Set B -
Sew a light background 2 1/2" x 22" strip to both edges of a print 2 1/2" x 22" strip. Cut the strip set into (4) 2 1/2" x 6 1/2" rectangles.

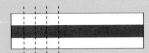

Strip Set C -
Sew a print 2 1/2" x 22" strip to both edges of a light background 6 1/2" x 22" strip. Cut the strip set into (8) 2 1/2" x 10 1/2" rectangles.

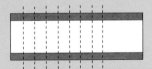

Cut the remaining 6 1/2" x 22" light background strip into (8) 2 1/2" x 6 1/2" rectangles.

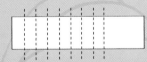

Make (4) Nine-Patch blocks with (2) rectangles from Strip Set A and (1) from Strip Set B.

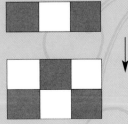

Sew a 2 1/2" x 6 1/2" rectangle to two opposite sides of each of the (4) Nine-Patch blocks.

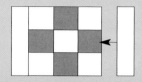

Sew a rectangle from Strip C to the top and bottom of each of the Nine-Patch units.

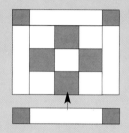

Appliqué Blocks

Choose your favorite appliqué method and prepare your templates for appliqué.

Appliqué the full lemon design onto the 11 1/2" square. Measure your Framed Nine-Patch blocks. If your seams were sewn with a consistent 1/4", the blocks will measure 10 1/2" square. Trim the appliqué block so it is the same size as your pieced blocks.

Putting it all together

Because the quarter-square triangles have raw bias edges, I suggest the quilt top be constructed before adding the appliqué to the triangles.

Sew a triangle to (2) opposite sides of two of the Framed Nine-Patch blocks. Align the corners and sew with the Nine-Patch on top as the fabric moves over the feed dogs of your sewing machine to avoid stretching

the bias edge. The units will look like the diagram below. Press the seam allowances toward the triangles, taking care to avoid touching the iron to the raw bias edge of the triangle.

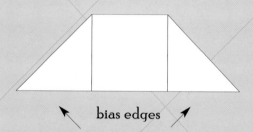

bias edges

Sew (2) Framed Nine-Patch blocks to opposite sides of the appliqué block. Press the seam allowances toward the appliqué block.

Sew the two rows containing the triangles to the top and bottom of the appliqué row. The opposing seam allowances will allow you to snug the intersections.

When you have sewn the top together, it is safe to add the appliqué to the triangles using the pattern on page 137.

Sandwich the quilt top and backing and batting. Baste using your favorite method and quilt, letting your aesthetic sense guide you. I recommend you quilt around each appliqué shape and then add a crosshatch in the background to make the appliqué stand out. The Framed Nine-Patch blocks lend themselves to a crosshatch, as well.

I recommend a batting with a very low loft if you will be using your quilt to top a table.

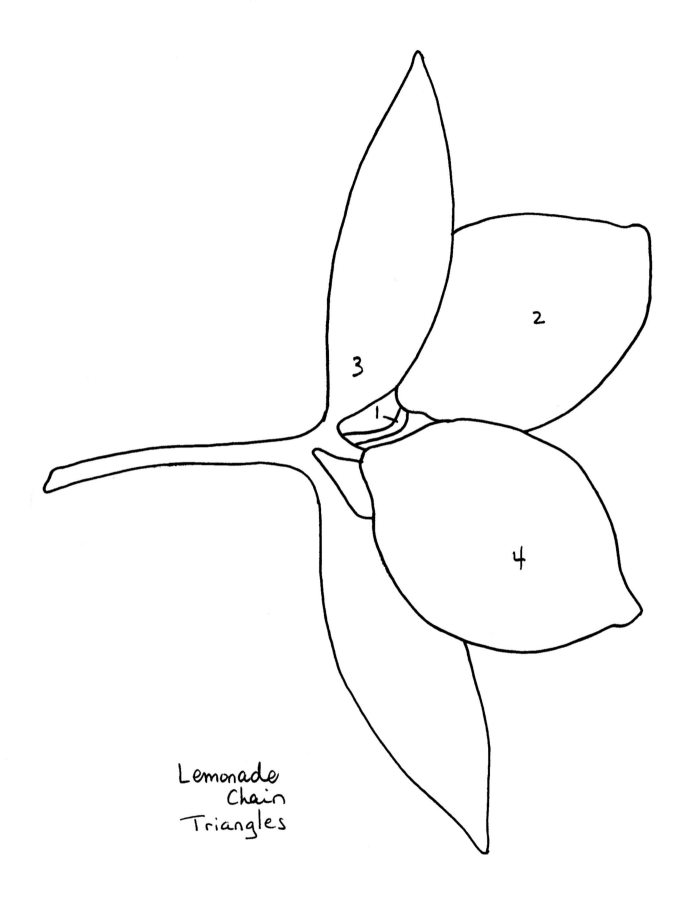

Lemonade
Chain
Triangles

"Pyramid of Fruit" Table Topper
45" on a side
Made by Barbara Fife, Overland Park, KS, 2004

"PYRAMID OF FRUIT" Table Topper

46" on each side

Fabric required:

- 1/4 yard of each of 6 neutral prints for the background and binding
- Assorted scraps for appliqué
- 1 1/4 yards for backing
- 52" x 50" piece of batting

Constructing the appliqué background

Cut all the strips from the width of the fabric, selvage to selvage, unless otherwise noted.

Because two of the three sides of every one of these pieces will be on the bias, I find it easier to stabilize the fabric before making my first cut. I recommend you starch and press all of the background prints before rotary cutting. In fact I heavily starch them. I want my strips to be very stiff. This will greatly aid in sewing as well as rotary cutting.

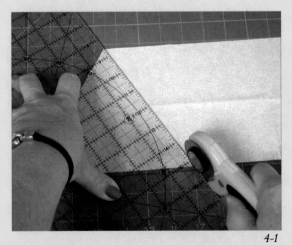

4-1

Cut a 5 3/4" strip from each of the neutral prints. Each strip will yield 11 triangles.

You'll need 64 to complete the quilt top.

Using a rotary ruler with a 60-degree mark, cut triangles from the strip. (4-1)

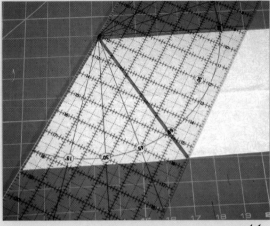

4-1a

You will need to turn the ruler upside down for each alternate triangle. (4-1a) Discard the partial triangle pieces from the ends of the strip.

You may wish to arrange the triangles on a design wall so no two triangles that touch are the same fabric, or you may wish to just mix all of the triangles and pull them randomly. On other occasions I might even suggest placing the triangles randomly in a paper bag, but because the fabric has been starched I would avoid it this time. Your personality, whether spontaneous or controlled, will determine your method of arranging the triangles. Arrange them as you like.

Row 1 has 15 triangles, 8 are "base triangles" and 7 are on point. Begin by matching two triangles, right sides together and sew with a 1/4" seam allowance. Make a perpendicular clip in the center of the seam allowance to the stitching without actually cutting the thread. Press one half of the seam away from the tip of the triangle. Because both triangles have tips, you will be pressing the seam allowance in opposite directions. (4-2)

A word about pressing: because each of the triangles has two bias edges, it is very important you are careful with your pressing. It is extremely important you set the iron down on the fabric and lift it right up. That is pressing. If you move the iron across the fabric, you will pull the fabric and distort the shape, and you will be ironing, not pressing.

Add a third triangle, again matching the side and placing them right sides together. Sew a 1/4" seam allowance, clip in the center and again press the seam allowance away from the tip of the triangles. Remember, you want to make sure you are always pressing away from the points. The only way you can accomplish this is to press the one seam in two directions. Clipping the center of the seam will allow you to do this.

Continue adding triangles in this manner until you have (15) triangles to complete the row.

4-2

Row 2 has (13) triangles. Each of the rows following has two fewer triangles than the previous row. The 15th row has just the one triangle.

When you have constructed the rows, sew them together. Begin with the longest row and add the next shorter row on top. Continue in this manner until you are adding the last triangle to the top row of the quilt top.

Pressing the seam allowances carefully is important to maintain the shape of your quilt top. Be gentle. It really won't matter which direction you press, as you will face plenty of intersecting seams either way.

To eliminate bulk, some quilters will press the seams open instead of in one direction or the other. Depending on the fabric you choose, the pressing will be up to you. A thicker fabric will require being pressed open while a thinner fabric, such as batik, will allow you to press to one side.

Adding the appliqué

Use the method of your choice for appliqué. Choose three of the fruit patterns or just one and place the designs in the corners. This will leave the center free for a bowl or flower arrangement without covering up the appliqué. Barb Fife used the oranges, yellow apples and the plums when she made the sample, but you are certainly not limited to those three patterns.

If you hand appliqué you can easily cut the background out from behind the appliqué so the bulk of the seams won't show through. If you machine appliqué with fusible web, consider cutting the center from the fusible within 1/4" from the tracing line before fusing to the fabric, leaving the center of the shape free of the fusible. (4-3) This will allow you to later cut the background out from behind the appliqué.

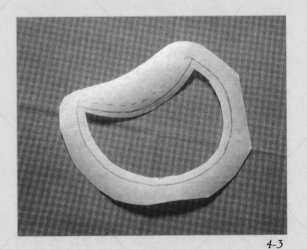

4-3

Finishing

Baste the quilt top, batting and backing in your favorite method. Quilt the sandwich, letting your aesthetic sense guide you. I recommend you quilt around each of the appliqué shapes to define them and then quilt the background. You can use an over-all pattern, such as the Baptist Fan or you can let the seams be your guide, quilting in the ditch or 1/4" inside the seams.

You have enough neutral fabric left over to cut (4) 2 1/2" x 40" strips from three different prints for the binding. You also have enough to make your binding even scrappier by cutting (6) 2 1/2" x 20" strips from the six different prints.

Sew the strips together, end to end, on a 45-degree angle. Press the seams open and trim to 1/4." Then press the long strip in half the full length, wrong side in. Remember to miter your corners and stitch those miters since the corners will be a sharper point. (4-4)

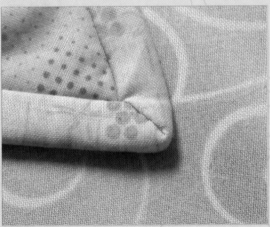

4-4

"Oranges" Chenille Pillow
16" x 16"
Made by Kathy Delaney,
Overland Park, KS, 2004

"Green Apples"
Chenille Pillow
16" x 16"
Made by Kathy Delaney,
Overland Park, KS, 2004

"IT'S GREEN APPLES AND ORANGES" Chenille Pillows
(2) 16" pillows

Fabric required:
- 1/2 yard prequilted muslin (This is a commercial product, consisting of muslin layers with two layers of needle punched batting in between and quilted in a chevron design in rows over the full surface.)
- 1 1/2 yards muslin for pillow backing and binding, pre-washed
- 1/4 yard print for binding if you wish instead of using muslin as in the samples
- Scraps for appliqué
- 1/2 yard light paper-backed fusible web
- (2) 16" pillow forms

Begin by stitching around an 18" square of the prequilted muslin, about 1/8" from the edge. Then stitch through the V's of the chevrons that were prequilted into the fabric from edge to edge. (4-5) This will break the zigzag quilting into five columns.

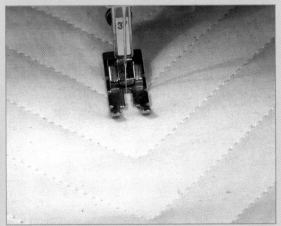

4-5

Trace the Orange pattern and the Yellow Apple pattern onto a sheet of 8 1/2" x 11" paper. Trace the individual appliqué shapes of the Orange block and the Apple block onto the paper side of the fusible web. (This time you will not trace the design as a complete picture as described for needleturn appliqué.) You may wish to reverse the patterns before tracing the shapes onto the fusible web by turning your traced patterns over and retracing the lines. This will give you a mirror image of the design. Fusible appliqué will make a mirror image of the pattern if you trace the patterns just as they are. I don't think it matters to the project if the appliqué ends up being a mirror image.

Cut around the appliqué shapes, about 1/2" outside the drawn line, with paper scissors. Fuse the web to the wrong side of your appliqué fabrics, following the heat setting directions that came with your fusible web product. Cut on the drawn lines and then peel the paper backing away.

Place a Teflon coated appliqué sheet over the appliqué pattern on your ironing board and layer the appliqué on the sheet, using the pattern as your guide. (4-6) With your iron set per the instructions that came with your fusible web, press the appliqué to the appliqué sheet. Let it cool and carefully peel the appliqué composition from the sheet and transfer it to the prequilted muslin, centering it as you wish.

4-6

Stitch around the appliqué with your sewing machine set on a straight stitch, zigzag stitch, a decorative stitch or a buttonhole stitch. You may use a contrasting thread or a matching thread of your choosing.

With a pair of scissors, cut through the top three layers (muslin and two layers of batting) of the quilted material between the rows of stitching, stopping before you cut through any stitching. Be very careful that you don't let your scissors cut through the bottom layer of muslin. (4-7)

Agitate the cut material in a washtub of water and then dry in the dryer to make the chenille "bloom" and the material shrink. Measure the chenille. On the uncut side, draw a 17" square if your chenille did not shrink. I don't recommend trimming

4-7

until after the backing has been added. (When I made the sample, the chenille shrunk just to 17" square so I didn't have to trace anything.)

From the muslin, cut (2) 17" x 14" rectangles. On one of the 14" sides fold the edge in 1" and press. Fold again 1" and top stitch to secure. Repeat with the other rectangle.

Place one of the rectangles on the backside of the chenille, aligning the raw edges or with the traced line if you had to draw the perimeter of the 17" square. The wrong side of the hemming should be against the back of the chenille, and will run across the center area of the square. Place the second rectangle on the backside of the chenille, matching the raw edges with the traced line or the edge of the chenille if you didn't have to trace a line. The two rectangles will overlap in the center. (4-8) Pin around the edge to secure, making sure to remove the pins as you stitch the binding.

4-8

you may place a 16" pillow form inside and consider your pillow complete!

Sew 1/4" in from the raw edge all the way around the entire square. Trim away the excess chenille.

Cut 2 1/4" strips from the remainder of the muslin or the binding print that you chose. You will only need two strips cut selvage to selvage. (I cut (4) 2 1/2" x 22" strips from a fat quarter for the samples.) Sew the two strips together, end-to-end, on a 45-degree line. Press the seam open and trim a 1/4" seam allowance. Press the strip in half the full length of the strip.

Bind the pillow as you would any quilt. I find it very helpful to use an even feed foot while sewing on the binding. Cut the excess chenille away before turning the binding to the back and stitching, if you have any. If the binding, when folded to the back is deeper than 1/4", take extra care that you don't stitch through more than the backing or your pillow form won't fit nicely. Once the binding is complete,

"Tropical Lemons" Pillow
18" x 18"
Made by Gloria Donohue, Olathe, KS, 2004.

"TROPICAL LEMONS" Pillow
18" Square

Fabric needed:

- (1) fat quarter print for the appliqué design
- 5/8 yard for background and pillow backing
- 5/8 yard muslin to back the pillow front
- 1/4 yard for binding
- 18" pillow form
- 22" x 22" piece of low loft batting

Appliqué

You may choose your favorite method of appliqué, but following is an easy way to accomplish Hawaiian style blocks with the sewing machine.

Remember making paper cut snowflakes when you were a kid? Begin by cutting an 18" square of freezer paper. Fold the paper as shown in the steps below:

4-9b

4-9c

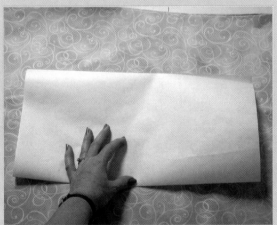
4-9a

4-9d

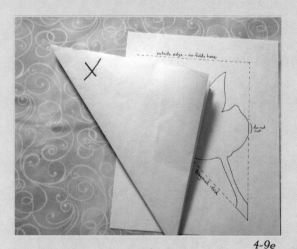

4-9e

4-11

Mark a small X on the top surface. (4-9e) When you open up the folded paper, you won't be able to recognize the same surface if you don't mark it. (4-10)

4-10

Trace the appliqué design found on page 151 onto the surface you marked. Align the edges as they are labeled on the design.

Refold the paper and staple the layers on the INSIDE of the appliqué shape. This will keep all the layers from slipping as you cut on the lines you traced. (4-11)

When you have completed the cutting, carefully open the paper "snowflake" template. Trim your fat quarter print to measure 18" square. Fold the fabric in half and finger press the center crease. Unfold, turn the fabric a quarter turn and fold in half again and finger press the center crease. Align the template on the fabric using the center creases as your guide to match the center creases on your template. The shiny side of the template should be against the right side of the fabric. Iron the template to the print. Your iron should be set to the wool setting with no steam. If you find that your freezer paper does not hold, raise the temperature of the iron to the cotton setting. If your iron runs cooler, you need to use the hotter setting. If the freezer paper template loosens while you are working, you can iron it again to secure.

From the background fabric cut a 20" square and finger press the center creases as you did previously. (Save the strips that you remove to finish the pillow.) Center the appliqué print with the template onto the right side of the background fabric. The wrong side of the print will be on top of the right side of the background. Place a few pins near the outside edges and a few in the template to secure the two layers of fabric. Make sure no pins intersect the edge of the template.

Thread your sewing machine with a thread that blends with the appliqué print. The closer you match the thread, the more the stitches will be hidden.

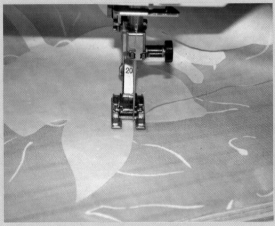

4-12

With a straight stitch, sew through both layers of fabric right next to the paper template. Do not sew through the paper. Sew next to all edges of the template. Gloria found it helpful to use an open-toed foot so she could see where she was sewing. (4-12)

Carefully remove the paper template from the fabric. With small scissors (I like to use the 4" knife-edge embroidery scissors)

cut the excess print away right next to the stitching. Avoid poking the background with your scissors while cutting as close to the stitching as possible.

Now you're ready for the fun part. Choose a decorative stitch on your sewing machine. It can be lacy or a satin stitch or just a simple zigzag stitch. You'll want to use a thread that contrasts with the appliqué and will add another design element. Stitch the edges of your appliqué, making sure to secure the "raw" edges and cover your previous stitching. You may find you need to stabilize the appliqué before you stitch. You may use a tear away product or a water-soluble stabilizer of your choosing. While freezer paper also works well, remember the paper will remain under the stitches.

I have also done this same technique couching a decorative thread over the edges instead of sewing a decorative stitch. I even added beads to dress the whole thing up! (4-13)

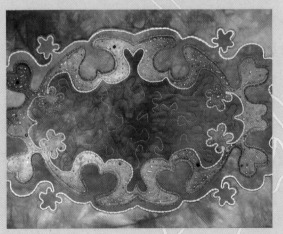

4-13

Once all the stitching is complete, you're ready to quilt. Treat your appliqué just as you would a big quilt. Layer the muslin, batting and appliqué in your favorite method and quilt. Hawaiian style includes echo quilting around the appliqué. Don't feel limited to echo quilting if you prefer another style.

Once the quilting is complete, trim your little quilt to measure 18 1/2" x 18 1/2" and set aside while you prepare the pillow back.

Putting it all together

Refer to the "Chenille Pillow" for instructional photographs, beginning on page 142.

Cut (2) 18 1/2" x 15" rectangles from the pillow backing. Fold one long edge, wrong side in, 1" and then another 1" and machine stitch to secure. Repeat with the second rectangle.

With wrong sides together, place one of the rectangles onto the bottom edge of your quilt. Align the raw edges. The finished edge will run across the center portion of the quilt back but will only cover a little over half of the back of the quilt. Place the second rectangle in the same way, covering the upper half of the quilt. The finished edges will overlap in the middle. Place a few pins in the interior of the rectangles to secure while you add the binding. You may want to stay-stitch about 1/8" from the raw edge all around the edge. This will keep the back pieces from shifting while you are adding the binding since you will be stitching with the other side facing up.

Cut (2) 2" strips from the binding fabric, cutting from selvage to selvage. Sew the two strips together at one end with a 45-degree seam. Press open and remove the excess seam allowance. Press the strip in half, wrong side in, along the full length of the strip.

Bind your pillow as you would any finished quilt, taking care that you only sew a 1/4-inch seam allowance. If your seams are a little more than 1/4" you will want to cut your binding strips 2 1/4" wide. With the binding in place, your pillow cover is complete.

I like to place a little extra fiberfill in the corners of my pillow cover before adding the pillow form to give my pillows a little more body in the corners. Slip the pillow form into the back of the pillow cover through the opening in the back. If you find the back opening gaps open, you might consider sewing a snap or a hook and loop button to the center of the overlap to secure the closure. Usually I have no need for either.

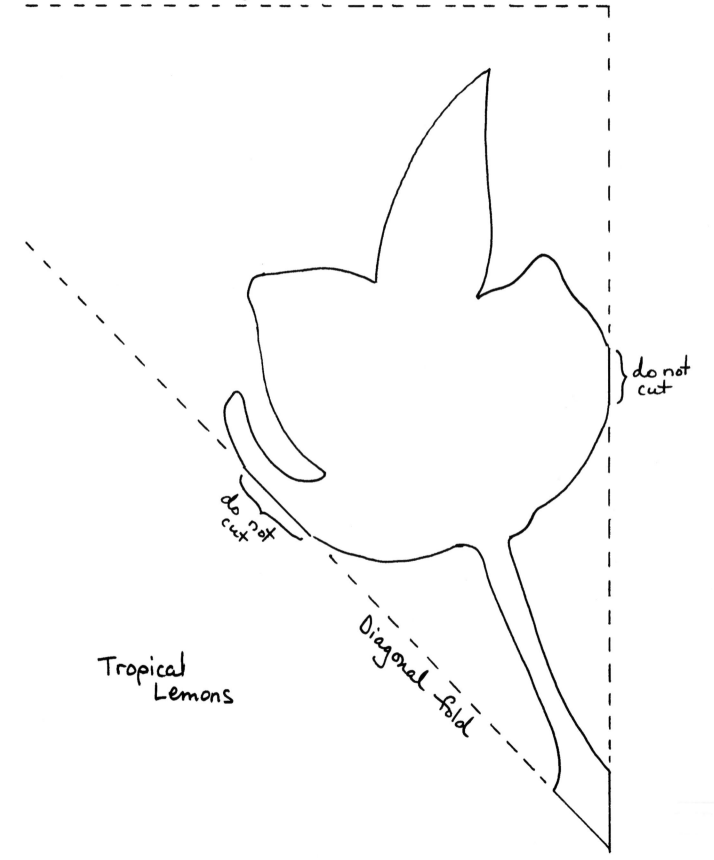

outside edge – no folds here

do not cut

do not cut

Diagonal fold

Tropical Lemons

CHAPTER 5
THE GALLERY

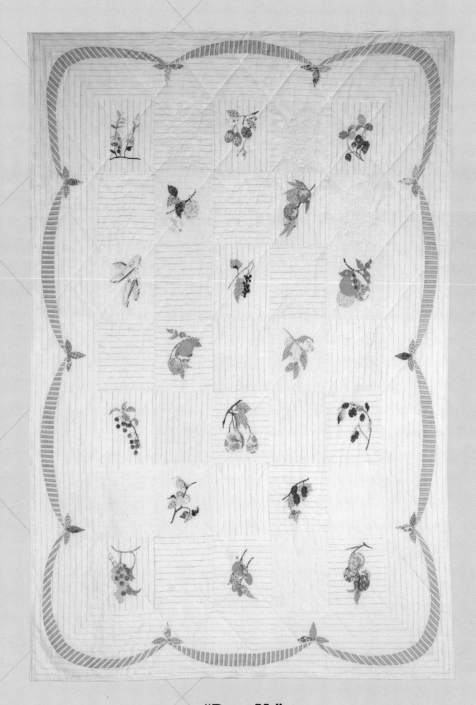

"Deja Vu"

70" x 103"

Made by Tresa Jones, Seneca, KS, 2004.

Tresa used no reproduction fabrics making this quilt.

"Rich Bounty"
29" x 43"
Made by Donna Howard, Watertown, SD, 2004,
framed by Penny LaBore of Watertown

"Fruit of the Vine"
29" x 43"
Made by Donna Howard, Watertown, SD, 2004,
framed by Penny LaBore of Watertown

"Moon Ripened"
25" x 36"
Made by Emily G. Senuta, Overland Park, KS, 2004

"Thankful for Blessings"
"19 1/2" x 38 1/2"
Made by Jeanne Poore, Overland Park, KS, 2004.

"Remembering Frugal Times"
41" x 41"
Made by Linda Birch Mooney, Shawnee, KS, 2004. The quilt was made using basket blocks
and fan blades made in the 1930's by Mrs. John Harper of Frankfurt, KS.

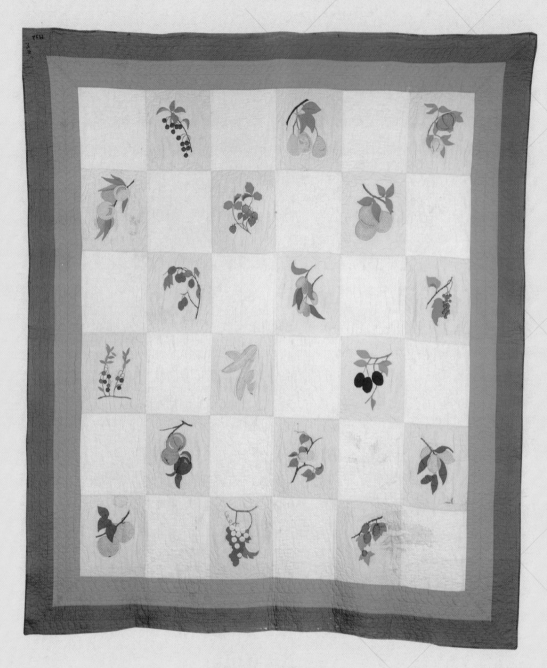

"Horn of Plenty"
69" x 78"
Made by Madeline Narron, dated 1932.
Owned by Deanna Spencer, Overland Park, KS.

"Horn of Plenty for a New Century"
83" x 80"
Made by Kathy Delaney, Overland Park, KS;
quilted by The Legler Barn Quilters, Lenexa, KS, 2004.

"Fruit Squared"
Made by Kathy Berner, Prairie View, KS, 2004.

"Batik Grapes"
20 1/2" x 24"
Made by Cathy Audley,
Overland Park, KS., 2004

"Bobbin Work Grapes"
15" x 18"
Made by Cathy Audley
Overland Park, KS. 2004

"Kumquat Lace"
29" x 29"
Made by Linda Kilpatrick, DeSoto, KS, 2004.

BIBLIOGRAPHY:

"Eveline Foland" by Louise O. Townsend, Quilter's Newsletter Magazine, April 1985

"Happy Endings - Finishing the Edges of Your Quilt" by Mimi Deitrich, That Patchwork Place, 1987

"Star Quilts II" by the staff of The Kansas City Star, Kansas City Star Books, 2000

"Christmastime in Kansas City - the Story of the Season" by Monroe Dodd, Kansas City Star Books, 2001

"Hearts and Flowers - Hand Appliqué from Start to Finish" by Kathy Delaney, Kansas City Star Books, 2002

"A Heartland Album - More Techniques in Hand Appliqué" by Kathy Delaney, Kansas City Star Books, 2003

"Making History - the 20th Century", Number 5, March 2003, Barbara Brackman

"The Basics - An Easy Guide to Beginning Quiltmaking" by Kathy Delaney, Kansas City Star Books, 2004

KANSAS CITY STAR QUILT BOOKS